"This is
Judy Woodruff
at the
White House"

Judy Woodruff
with Kathleen Maxa

"This is
Judy Woodruff
at the
White House"

Judy Woodruff
with Kathleen Maxa

ADDISON-WESLEY PUBLISHING COMPANY
Reading, Massachusetts • Menlo Park, California
London • Amsterdam • Don Mills, Ontario • Sydney

Library of Congress Cataloging in Publication Data

Woodruff, Judy.
   "This is Judy Woodruff at the White House."

   Includes index.
      1. Woodruff, Judy.   2. Journalists—United States—
Biography.   I. Maxa, Kathy.   II. Title.
PN4874.W693A36   1982   070′.92′4 [B]   82-6865
ISBN 0-201-08850-9

ISBN 0-201-08850-9

   BCDEFGHIJ-DO-85432

Second Printing, November 1982

For Albert and Jeffrey,
the two men in my life
who mean everything to me

Acknowledgements

I owe an enormous debt of gratitude to NBC News, for giving me the opportunity to write this book. Among those whose time and contributions were especially important are my parents, William and Anna Lee Woodruff, and Bob Brennan, who gave me my first reporting job. Others who were indispensible, either because they provided information, or were kind enough to critique the early manuscript, were: Joan Barone, Phyllis Cahoon, Lou Cannon, Jim Doyle, Margot Dunlap, Ellen Ehrlich, Charles Ferris, Jim Lee, Martin Linsky, Andrea Mitchell, John Palmer, Leroy Powell, Michael Putzel, Michael Robinson, Greg Schneiders, John Sears, Anne Shields, Mark Shields, Susan Tannenbaum, and Jeani Wilson. Many of the insights are theirs and, alas, all the oversights are mine. A special thanks to the following, for speaking or writing so well that I have quoted from them liberally: George Reedy, Roger Mudd, Tom Wicker, Hodding Carter, and Sidney Blumenthal.

The idea for this book emanated from a diary I wrote for the April 26, 1981, Washington *Post Magazine*; the inspirations and guiding forces behind that piece were Nick Lemann and Stephen Petranek. The book itself benefited from the superb research of Darci Vanderhoff. Special thanks are due two talented and supportive people: Harriet Rubin, my editor at Addison-Wesley, and my agent, Esther Newberg of International Creative Management.

Above all, I am especially grateful to Kathleen Maxa, who so often managed to find sense and coherence in my disjointed thoughts.

On a more personal level, I cannot repay the hours Sabine

Acknowledgements

Laborde spent watching Jeffrey. And I owe more thanks than words can express to my husband, Albert Hunt, for his patience, his excellent suggestions, and his confidence in me.

Finally, I feel a special bond with the pioneer women in television, starting with Pauline Frederick. They made it so much easier for those of us in the business today.

Judy Woodruff
WASHINGTON, D.C.
APRIL *15, 1982*

Contents

Preface

Even in the best of times, the television news business is crazy. The competition is fierce, the money at stake is huge, and the potential impact is heady and sobering. And even in the best of times, covering the White House is crazy. The constraints are rigid, the demands are relentless, and the stories are complex.

But combine the business of television news with the business of covering the president of the United States and the result can be chaotic. Toss in what has been called the fine madness of Washington, a town filled with people driven by ambition and a lust for power, and you have summarized my job.

I report on the White House for NBC network news. When the President acts, confers, travels, or blinks, it's my job to be there and to provide reports for NBC's 530 radio and more than 200 television affiliates. As a White House correspondent, I have a close-up view of the President at work and at play. I see history in the making and, in a sense, I contribute to a first draft of history by reporting the actions and statements of the President.

Working for a major news network means I wield a measure of power. Seventeen million potential voters rely on my "NBC Nightly News" reports to inform them about the President and his policies. More than 100 million Americans rely primarily on television for their news. Those numbers mean that most of my phone calls to White House officials are returned. But they also mean that I have an enormous responsibility to be accurate, thorough, and fair.

The daily news-vigil reporters keep at the White House is an extension of the people's right to know how their government works. The reporter's job is to provide the public with that information. Gathering those facts is a highly competitive pursuit. I share the job with two other NBC correspondents, and we share the beat with hundreds of other reporters. After the federal government and tourism, the news media constitute the capital city's largest industry. More than three thousand newspaper, periodical, and broadcast journalists work in Washington. Of those, less than 100 regularly cover the White House. For many of them, the White House assignment represents the high point of a distinguished career; for others, it's a stepping stone to media stardom as a nationally syndicated newspaper columnist or network television news anchor. Tom Wicker, the late Peter Lisagor, Tom Brokaw, Dan Rather, and John Chancellor are some of the former White House correspondents who have made the leap to the top of their profession. For others, the White House beat has provided a one-way ticket to the journalistic boondocks.

Since 1977, the White House has been my second home. My office there is a tiny cubicle littered with press releases that seem to grow like dandelions after a spring rain. My life is ruled by the telephone—which may ring at any moment with an order from an editor, or a news development that I must drop all else to pursue—and by the President's schedule. He wants to go to Plains, Georgia, over Thanksgiving weekend; I go along and spend Thanksgiving in a motel reporting on the President's holiday at home with his family. He flies to Chicago to make a speech; I fly there, too, to report what the President said. He makes a pilgrimage for peace to the Middle East; I go to Cairo and Jerusalem with him and cover his meetings with Arab and Israeli leaders.

Whether the President is on the road or at the White House, a large part of my job is done over the telephone, talking to his advisors, aides, and others who might be able to provide clues about the man in the Oval Office and the decisions before him. For, while viewers watching me reporting from the White House front lawn would naturally assume that I have ready access to the president and his men, the fact is that access is very tightly controlled. Although reporters and aides work under the same roof in the West Wing of the White House, no reporter is free to roam the halls or drop in unannounced on a presidential aide, and there are no informal gatherings around the water cooler. My access to the President himself is even more limited. Some days I don't even catch a glimpse of him; most days I see him for only a few minutes while he poses for network television and news photographers' cameras during "photo opportunities" before and after his meetings.

White House reporters and White House officials coexist in a state of some mutual distrust and frequently pursue conflicting goals. I try, to the best of my ability, to present an accurate picture of the President and his policies. Sometimes my reports make the President and his men look good; sometimes they don't. The aim of White House officials, obviously, is to present the most flattering image of the president and his administration. Often, in their eyes, favorable stories are fair; unfavorable ones are unfair.

This is a story of what it is like to work in Washington in times when crises seem to have become routine. It is not meant to be a definitive account of how Washington operates—that is a topic for someone far more experienced than I. Nor is it an examination of the television news business—that, too, I leave to the experts.

Indeed, I had reservations about writing a book at all. One of the people I admire most in our business is NBC's John Chancellor, who, the *Wall Street Journal* recently noted, has avoided "sliding into the costume jewelry world of celebrity," as he "has not had the details of his private life, his career, his opinions of his career or his salary negotiations slathered across the 'lifestyle' sections of America's newspapers and

magazines." Like Chancellor, I have real qualms about journalists, myself included, writing or talking in public about the
purely personal side of their lives. To the extent I deal with the
personal aspects of my life in this book, the chief aim is to
provide a clearer picture of the pressures and pleasures of my
profession.

Mine is the perspective of a relative newcomer to a very
tough business. I've had to contend with the relentless insecurity
of big-time journalism and the extra insecurity that comes with
being a woman in the mostly male club that rules my profession and the political institutions I have covered. There
was a time in television news when a woman would never have
thought of covering national politics. To be a local "weather
girl," which was my first assignment on camera, or a women's
feature reporter were more realistic aspirations when I started
in television ten years ago. The business of reporting on government, like the business of governing, was the province of
men. Today at the White House I am joined by Ann Compton
of ABC, Andrea Mitchell of NBC, and Lesley Stahl of CBS.
A number of women network correspondents have moved from
the White House to other beats. And more and more women
have been assigned to cover the State Department, Capitol
Hill, and national political campaigns and conventions.

These chapters are intended to provide a glimpse behind
the camera, beyond the precisely timed scripts and carefully
arranged lights that are part of television news. While covering
the White House for NBC carries a measure of glamour and
fame, and opens the door to speaking engagements and state-
dinner invitations, the day-to-day work of a correspondent is
marked by small victories and bigger frustrations.

This is also the story of a single career woman who recently
became a wife and working mother. My husband, Al Hunt, is
a reporter in the Washington bureau of the *Wall Street
Journal* who specializes in national politics. As I write this,

my son, Jeffrey, is a six-month-old night owl who specializes in stealing the show.

Al's and my courtship was defined by, as the television cliché goes, circumstances beyond our control—deadlines imposed by fast-breaking stories. Our life is still like that: bologna lunches eaten on the run and fast-food carryout for dinner. NBC provides a generous expense account that permits me to take top White House officials to fancy lunches. What my job *doesn't* provide very often is the time for those lunches.

Although this book most definitely is not an autobiography, woven through it is the story of how one woman blends a demanding job with the responsibility of running a house and being a wife and mother. Some women may be able to forget about their families and homes and focus totally on their jobs when they are at work. I'm not one of them. During White House press briefings I often worry about whether there's enough food in the refrigerator for dinner, and while I'm fixing dinner I worry about preparing for the next day's interviews.

I love both my work and my family. I hope that first sentiment is clear even when I describe the pressures and strictures of television news. I continue to find television reporting as exciting as it is sometimes exasperating. And I hope the second sentiment is obvious to my husband and son, even when I can't make it home for dinner. Given a choice, I'd prefer hearing about their day to listening to the President toast a visiting head of state.

Countdown: March 30, 1981

When the alarm sounded that rainy March morning at the usual hour of half-past six, it took every bit of discipline I could muster to resist the urge to roll over and go back to sleep. At least it's Monday, I told myself, trying to look on the bright side of a gray day. Mondays at the White House are usually slow and often predictable.

This Monday promised to be one of those rare days when I could almost guess the lead to my story for "Nightly News" before I covered it: "President Reagan appealed to workers to support his federal spending and tax-cut programs today in his first speech as President before a major labor group. . . ."

I never did broadcast that story, however. This was the day John Hinckley shot Ronald Reagan.

I was particularly tired that morning. Three months pregnant with my first child, I was only beginning to understand that I required more sleep than usual. Also, the weekend had been a long and hectic one. Friday night after work my husband and I gave a dinner party for a friend who was visiting from New York. Early Saturday morning I flew to Tampa, Florida, to speak to a women's civic group about covering the White House. From Tampa, I flew to Atlanta to visit an old girlfriend with whom I stayed the night. And from Atlanta, I flew to Washington on Sunday afternoon so that I could attend a performance by the Gridiron Club.

The Gridiron is a mostly male honorary fraternity of print journalists known mainly for its annual white-tie dinner wherein formality gives way to folderol as the Washington press establishment performs a series of satirical speeches, songs, and skits before the Washington political establishment, many of whom are the objects of parody. Traditionally, the President and his top aides attend to watch themselves hoisted high with their own political petards. This time, on a March weekend in 1981, Senator Daniel Patrick Moynihan, the Democrat from New York who is known for his eloquence and wry wit, "roasted" Ronald Reagan, the Republican who was once a Democrat.

"Back in 1962, when you resigned from Americans for Democratic Action, renounced the New Deal, and turned Republican," Moynihan had said, "all the press could figure out was that you wanted to make a living. Little did they suspect that the old mole was at work. . . . Who would have dreamed that you'd make it all the way to the White House and institute the basic plan to destroy the Republican Party *from within?*"

Because the Saturday gala dinner is for Gridiron members and their guests only, I attended a Sunday afternoon cocktail gathering held for the friends and family of members, one of whom is my husband, Al. Like many Washington institutions, the Gridiron dinner was a stag affair until 1975, when it bowed to pressure from women reporters who picketed several of the dinners and finally opened its doors to a select few female journalists such as Helen Thomas of UPI and columnist Mary McGrory. Broadcast reporters are still excluded.

I was curious to know how the newly elected President had responded to his ribbing by Moynihan, and I returned to Washington figuring that the Sunday affair would be buzzing with talk of the President's reaction. My curiosity was well rewarded. Reagan, I learned, had demonstrated his own adroit capacity for wit. The conservative President told the audience about his new Administration, "Sometimes the right hand doesn't know what the *far* right hand is doing."

Another Gridiron skit featured a character who bore a striking resemblance to Democratic Speaker of the House Tip O'Neill—only dressed as a bride—singing, "Honeymoon, it could last until June," referring to the newlywed affection between the ten-week-old Reagan Administration and official Washington.

I was told that the President and his press secretary, James Brady, laughed uproariously at the O'Neill impersonation. If the Gridiron were any indication, it seemed that the President and his spokesman were off to a rousing start in Washington.

That evening we attended a dinner party at the home of a political scientist friend, Austin Ranney of the American Enterprise Institute, a Washington think tank. It was an informal gathering of journalists, politicians, and academics. Naturally, the main topic of conversation was politics. The evening was as informative as it was entertaining, with United Nations Ambassador Jeane Kirkpatrick being bombarded with questions about her recent controversial meeting with South African officials despite the stated U.S. policy of limited contact with their government. We ended up staying later than we had intended. It was nearly midnight when I collapsed into bed, exhausted. I vowed I would never again try to cram so much into a single weekend, even though I knew I would. I'm happiest on a full schedule.

But, that Monday morning, I was looking forward to a routine day. And I was relieved that the only major event I had to cover was the President's speech at 2:00 before a conference of the AFL-CIO's Building and Construction Trades Department at the Washington Hilton Hotel. I knew about the speech in advance because the White House press office provides reporters with prior word of the President's schedule as a courtesy, so that we have as much time as possible to plot our coverage of the events the White House wants to see covered. This is one of the rare examples of the White House's interest coinciding with ours.

I also knew it was NBC's turn to cover the President's motorcade to the hotel. As a matter of course, whenever the President leaves the White House, and particularly when he is out in the open, the networks accompany him and the cameras are always rolling. The practice is sometimes ghoulishly referred to as the "death watch." We know that the President is more vulnerable physically when he is in public and that is why we go—just in case.

Even when our interests coincide, the extent to which the White House cooperates with us is limited. For logistical reasons, it's impossible for all three network crews and all nine White House correspondents regularly assigned to the President to accompany his motorcade every time he drives somewhere. Television coverage of the motorcade, therefore, is limited by the White House to a rotating group of reporters and crews called a "pool." The pool includes one network correspondent and crew, who later distribute a report and videotape footage to the other TV news organizations covering the White House.

Normally, motorcade pool duty is considered drudge work by reporters. The only advantage to the assignment is that it provides what may be one's sole opportunity to elicit a quote from the President that day. Many days the pool reporters may be the only journalists close enough to the President to address a question directly to him—usually as he is climbing in and out of his limousine—or to catch him making an impromptu remark. The pool report normally doesn't produce anything newsworthy or noteworthy, however, which is why reporters don't relish the assignment.

But on a rainy day, motorcade pool duty is a bonus. I knew

I wouldn't have to walk out to Pennsylvania Avenue in a downpour and pray for a scarce taxi to drive me from the White House to the President's speech at the Hilton. Pool reporters are chauffeured door-to-door in two gray press vans which are included in the President's motorcade so that they can follow him every step of the way.

All in all, Monday was shaping up as a fairly easy day when I arrived at my booth in the White House press room about nine that morning. I read the morning newspapers. I phoned a couple of White House aides to discuss the President's speech—what he was expected to say, why he was saying it, and why he had chosen this time. I also phoned an official of the Building and Construction Trades conference to ask how Reagan happened to be invited to speak and how the group had reacted to his proposed economic package, which the President was expected to tout in his speech. Then I set to work arranging interviews for a two-hour documentary on Reagan's first 100 days in office. I was one of several correspondents contributing to the special NBC television report and my assignment was to look at how the Reagan White House worked.

I planned to focus on the Reagan triumvirate—counselor to the President Edwin Meese, Chief of Staff James Baker, and Deputy Chief of Staff Michael Deaver. A former prosecutor who has worked for Reagan since the ex-movie star was elected governor of California, Meese is the earnest policy and issues man who is sometimes called Reagan's "synthesizer" because he is good at condensing information for the President's use in making decisions. Deaver, also a Californian, is an affable former public relations man who is personally the closest to the President of all his aides. Reporters called him the "keeper of the body" because he makes sure that everything from Reagan's meals to his public appearances is arranged just the way the boss likes. Baker is the outsider and organizer. A hard-driving lawyer with a native Texas drawl, he is the only one among them whose political experience reaches beyond Ronald Reagan. Baker ran unsuccessfully for Texas attorney general in 1978, between managing both Gerald Ford's 1976 presidential campaign and George Bush's 1980 bid to win the Republican nomination over Reagan. Nevertheless, he caught the eye of the Reaganites, who brought him in for the general election campaign.

I also planned to focus on the Reagan White House's carefully orchestrated media relations, including a look at James Brady, the President's jovial and popular press secretary. Brady is a gentle man with a self-effacing sense of humor and an ursine physique that prompts him to refer to himself as "the bear." He was as comfortable with reporters as they were with him. But I knew that Brady was a shrewd player of the Washington media game and that he had earned his reputation as a P. T. Barnum among press secretaries when he worked on Capitol Hill.

Formerly press secretary to Senator William Roth, the Republican from Delaware who sponsored the Kemp-Roth tax-cut bill, Brady deserved much of the credit for ensuring that his boss received the credit due him. When Democrats sponsored an almost identical tax-cut amendment which threatened to co-opt the Republicans', Brady dubbed the bill "Son of Kemp-Roth" and came up with the idea of printing birth announcements heralding the arrival of this clone. Then he bought a box of cheap cigars, which he wrapped with tiny bands bearing the GOP elephant symbol. The next day, when Republican leaders held a press conference to remind the world that Kemp-Roth was a Republican invention, Senator Roth burst into the room with a box of cigars and copies of the birth announcements, which he passed out to reporters. A photograph of Roth striking a cigar-chomping pose made the front page of the *Washington Post*. "It was a classic case of the Republicans using a hyped-up media event to make a political point," said Chris Wallace, who was there for NBC. "Had they held a straight, conservative, respectable news conference, they wouldn't have gotten any attention at all."

At the White House Brady used his skills more subtly, but just as effectively, to try to cajole reporters into reflecting the image of the President and his Administration that he wanted portrayed—strong, capable, always in control.

Even though it meant extra work without extra time in which to do it, I was excited about the documentary because it offered me the opportunity to say something more about the White House than "Here's the news," which is all the typical minute-and-a-half "Nightly News" broadcast provides time for. I was beginning to feel pressured by my deadline, however, which was just three weeks away, so I was thankful for the chance afforded by this rare quiet morning to squeeze in a few calls. Although I often try to take advantage of slow news days by going to lunch with sources, I ate a turkey sandwich at my desk so that I would have more time to think about the documentary.

What was intriguing to me about the Reagan White House was that so far the triumvirate—Meese, Deaver, and Baker— had managed to share equal power and access to the President without tripping over each other's egos. No president in recent memory had succeeded in keeping his advisors from sniping at each other, much less in keeping them content to share power. I suspected that the reason why this President's men were working so harmoniously was that they had not yet been put to any major test in the ten-week-old Administration. So far the events and issues they had had to deal with had been relatively manageable ones. And although the test was just a few hours away, on the morning of the seventieth day of Ronald Reagan's presidency, it seemed that the honeymoon would last until June, just as the Gridiron's Tip O'Neill character had sung.

Shortly after one o'clock, I placed a routine call to the NBC bureau in Washington to find out if there had been any news developments that, as the pool reporter, I would be expected to try and ask the President about. Les Kretman, the assignment editor, answered the call and told me of the latest development in Poland's volatile labor struggle—a strike had been called off. I made a mental note to ask the President for a reaction sometime during his outing.

At about 1:35, the reporters and photographers in the travel pool were escorted by a White House press aide to two gray vans parked outside the south door of the White House residence, where the NBC pool crew, cameraman Bill Powell and soundman John Levy, was already set up in the rain, ready to begin videotaping the President's departure through the van's sunroof. From inside the van, I watched the President emerge from the south door and, as the camera rolled, walk the ten or so feet to the 1972 black Lincoln Continental limousine emblazoned with presidential seals on the doors and decorated with an American flag and a President's flag on the front fenders. Reagan, who was wearing a blue suit with a white handkerchief in his pocket, was smiling. The thick gray clouds hanging overhead and the steady drizzle apparently had not dampened his spirits. An aide held the door of the car as the President climbed into the back of the limousine and my pool crew crouched down in the van with their gear. The motorcade started to move. But for the rain, they would have continued rolling throughout the drive.

The times when a president can discreetly slip away from the White House unannounced are rare. The most powerful man in the world serves under the ever-present threat of attack and the relentless scrutiny of reporters, conditions which he is powerless to change. Because every step he takes is measured by Secret Service bodyguards and monitored by reporters and television cameras, even a routine drive across town rivals Hannibal's crossing of the Alps, logistically speaking, and involves a week of planning and a caravan of cars to ferry the guards, aides, and reporters who accompany the President.

During an interview a few weeks earlier, Ronald Reagan had told the network correspondents that he sometimes felt like a bird in a gilded cage inside the White House. What he didn't say, but what unfortunately turned out to be all too true, is that outside the White House he is a sitting duck. Despite the extraordinary security measures the Secret Service takes to protect the President, his bodyguards have no illusions about the job that they do. They know that a determined, patient assassin can penetrate even the most carefully laid security plan. In the final analysis, their job is to make the possible as difficult as possible.

Whenever a president makes a public appearance, Secret Service agents visit the site a week in advance to case the building, examining everything from the entrance he will use to the corridors through which he will pass and the rooms where he will pause. They also map out a route for his motorcade to follow, noting whether there are any potential hazards along the way—a construction boom overhead, for example, or subway repairs being made below. "We know exactly what is going on along that route—beneath us and above us," is how one Secret Service agent put it.

The day of the event, hours before the president arrives at the scene, the Secret Service returns to the site to secure the area by checking for explosives and other hazards and investigating any overlook sights or roof tops where a sniper might lurk. Then they "seal off" the area, meaning that they monitor everyone who enters and leaves from that time on. Any sidewalk or other public area where the president will pass is normally roped off, too, and only authorized news people and security and White House staff are permitted behind the ropes. Lastly, they make sure that a specially reserved ambulance is waiting at every site the president visits.

Several minutes before the president's motorcade departs from the White House, a route car starts out along the same route to make sure that the local police are positioned and ready at each intersection to halt traffic until the motorcade has passed. Once the route car has radioed that everything is set, the motorcade proceeds, led by motorcycle policemen who peel off along the way as necessary to help stop traffic and then rejoin the motorcade. Next comes the pilot car, which carries armed Secret Service agents and an advance staff, whose job it is to get on the ground immediately before the president's car arrives at the destination point. The moment the president emerges from the car, the advance staff forms a shifting human shield around him.

Following the pilot car is the so-called "back up" car, which normally carries the President's personal doctor. Next is the president's car, which is specially outfitted with armor and bullet-proof glass and driven by a Secret Service agent trained in the most advanced techniques of defensive driving. He is joined in the front seat by a second agent. "Rawhide," as the Secret Service code named Reagan, sits in the rear.

A specially designed, partially armored, black stretch Cadillac usually follows the president's car. Loaded with submachine guns, rifles, and ammunition—which are carried out of sight but within quick reach of the agents inside—the vehicle is also outfitted with an opening in the front of the roof, a convertible-type top in the rear, and running boards. The running boards enable agents to hang on or jump out quickly when the vehicle is in motion.

A nondescript sedan, called the control car, is next. It carries the radio equipment that controls the motorcade's pace as the agents who have moved ahead secure the route on a block-by-block basis, and the ever-present military aide with the "football." The football is actually a black bag that contains top-secret military and communication codes that follow the president wherever he goes, to be used in the event of a national security crisis. The staff vehicle follows, carrying any White House aides who may be accompanying the president.

Then come the two press vans carrying the pool reporters, photographers, and television crew, followed by an ambulance. The ambulance is specially equipped with telemetry, an electrical process for transmitting to the nearest emergency room the vital signs of wounded passengers and any other relevant medical information before it arrives there.

The routine logistics of television coverage of a public appearance by the President are planned almost as thoroughly as his security protection. We, like the Secret Service, monitor every step the President takes to the extent that the Service permits. In addition to the pool reporter and crew, who are responsible for covering the President from the moment he leaves the White House until he arrives at his destination, each network typically assigns one or possibly two of its own crews. The day of Ronald Reagan's speech at the Hilton, NBC set up one crew near where the President's limousine would park, in order to videotape him from the instant he emerged from the car until he disappeared through the hotel door, at which point the pool was supposed to take over. Inside the ballroom where the President was to speak, a second crew was ready to begin rolling as soon as he entered the room and throughout his speech. Although I was not aware of it at the time, a third, roving NBC crew was also present on this day to photograph the President for the documentary in progress.

At precisely the scheduled time, 1:45, the President's limousine rolled out the south drive of the White House, followed by the rest of the motorcade, and turned onto 17th Street, passing the New Executive Office Building and continuing north up Connecticut Avenue toward the Washington Hilton, about eight blocks away. Through the window of the van I saw the last of the lunchtime crowd scurrying under umbrellas back to their offices in the concrete-and-glass high-rise buildings which line the busy avenue. A few of the pedestrians paused briefly to stare at the passing motorcade, but most continued on their way unmindful of the fuss. Washington generally regards presidential motorcades with less curiosity than other cities accord speeding ambulances. The only time the natives get excited is when a President's motorcade snarls or delays traffic.

Normally, Connecticut Avenue is clogged with traffic and even a short drive between the White House and the Hilton could take ten minutes. But because the police made sure that we had no other traffic or red lights to contend with, we made the trip in just five minutes. That's one advantage of traveling with the President. We arrived at the Hilton before 2:00 and pulled up under a concrete canopy at the T Street side entrance. A small cluster of people stood on the sidewalk across the street. Probably tourists, I thought, who had read in the newspapers about the President's scheduled appearance. Until the FBI determined that this was how John Hinckley knew where to find Ronald Reagan that day, Washington newspapers always published the President's daily agenda.

As soon as the motorcade stopped, I jumped out of the press van in time to see the President disappear through the VIP entrance to the hotel about twenty feet away from me. Although we ask the White House press office to permit the pool to be with the President every step of the way, they argue that, for security reasons, this isn't always possible. Apparently this was one of those times as several policemen blocked our way. Nice of them to tell me in advance, I thought, as I turned and raced through the lobby, down the stairs to the next level, and along the corridor to the International ballroom, where Mr. Reagan was to give his speech. As the pool reporter, I'm not supposed to let the President out of my sight. My crew and I are solely responsible for the television coverage of him until he enters the room to make his speech. At that point he be-come's everybody's story.

When I entered the ballroom the President had not yet ar-rived. I checked my watch and saw that it was nearly 2:00, when the speech was scheduled to begin. I knew I could depend on the President to be punctual, even if I couldn't depend on his aides to tell me which entrance he would use.

I took a seat in a press area, about twenty feet to the right of the President's podium, the closest I would be to the Presi-dent all day. At exactly 2:00, Reagan entered the room and was greeted by polite, but not enthusiastic, applause from the 3500 construction workers in attendance. Just as I had been told earlier by one of the White House staffers, the speech was basically a pitch for Reagan's economic program. In a line that drew one of the four rounds of applause that in-terrupted him, the President spoke of "just too many people" in the federal bureaucracy who believe "the billions of dollars raised from taxpayers belong to the government."

The speech ended about 2:20. Immediately, the White House press staff began moving the pool out so that we would be in position outside when the President left the hotel to get back in his car. My pool crew and I left the same way we had come in. Outside, the cluster of spectators who had greeted the President's arrival had swelled to maybe a hundred who now stood with reporters and television cameramen inside a roped-off area just ten feet from the President's car. The motorcade was still parked in the canopied driveway in the same order in which we had left it—first the President's limousine, about twenty feet from the VIP door; then the Secret Service follow-up car, the control car, the staff car, and the press van and ambulance.

As I rushed toward the press van, out of the corner of my eye I caught the President and his entourage of aides and security men coming out of the VIP door about forty feet from where I was standing. I wanted to ask the President a question about Poland and I figured this would be my only chance to do it. I started toward the President's car, but I realized that my pool crew was not with me. Without them to videotape the President's answer, there was no point in my asking the question. Ironically, this is the one time when technical difficulties, the bane of my job, may have saved my life. Instead of running over to the limousine, I stayed back. I saw the President pause, as he often does, to wave to the crowd, which was standing about ten feet away from him on the other side of a rope.

Then I heard the pop, pop—pop, pop, pop, pop. It sounded at first like firecrackers—muffled firecrackers. But suddenly the thought flashed: Nobody would be playing with firecrackers so close to the President. In that instant of realizing that the explosions I had heard were a fusillade of gunshots, my heart froze. A dozen images raced through my mind. I didn't know immediately where the shots had come from. The concrete canopy over my head was like an echo chamber which had distorted the sound of the shots so that it seemed as though they might have come from overhead.

I saw a Secret Service agent looking up at the roof of the gray office building across the street. I thought I might be in the line of fire. I heard a woman scream and people shouting, "Get back, get back." I half crouched and at the same time half craned to see what was going on. My instinct was to run for cover, but I didn't want to leave the President. I thought about being pregnant. What would it mean for the baby if I were hit?

Then I saw the puffs of smoke about forty feet away from me in the middle of the roped-off area. People were pushing and shouting as uniformed police converged on a man in the crowd, wrestling him to the ground. In the confusion, I couldn't see the President. All I saw was a jumble of bodies pile into

14

the back seat of the limousine and speed away. Then I saw the bodies on the sidewalk next to the staff car.

Michael Deaver, the deputy White House chief of staff, was running toward me, shouting, "Let's go, let's go," to the driver of the control car, which was parked next to me. As Deaver jumped into the back seat, I shouted to him, "Is the President hit? Is the President hit?" He didn't answer. But someone, whom I didn't recognize, replied confidently, "No, no. The President is all right."

My mind was racing now. For a split second, I considered jumping into the staff car with Deaver, but all the doors slammed shut, and there was no opportunity. I worried that even though the President was on his way back to the White House, that I should be, too. My job was to follow the President—wherever he was.

But three men in the President's entourage had been shot. And I wasn't certain whether any other NBC reporter had been on the scene to witness the shooting. I decided that I should stay there. I needed to find out who the wounded were and how badly they had been hurt and to try to determine whether or not the President had been wounded. The story was here. It seemed the right choice at the time. But it was a decision I would regret later when I learned that the President had in fact been hit.

As Deaver's car pulled away, I started running the twenty or so feet to where the wounded men lay on the sidewalk, obscured from my view now by a huddle of people. I heard someone say, "We're still not sure if there are any other gunmen in the area." It crossed my mind that we could all be surrounded by snipers, for all we knew. But I didn't have time to worry about such possibilities. I knew I had to determine who had been hit and get to a telephone.

Rocky Kuonen of the White House advance staff was running toward me to help police keep people back behind the ropes. He appeared dazed, as though he was still trying to comprehend what had happened. I grabbed his sleeve to stop him. "Are you sure Reagan was not hit?" I asked.

"I wasn't close enough," he said. "I don't know."

One of the men sprawled on the sidewalk was wearing a police uniform. The other two, dressed in business suits, were unrecognizable to me. One of them was lying on a grate, face down. His head was in a pool of blood which trickled across the grate and down the sidewalk toward the hotel entrance. His body was convulsing. I heard someone say that it was James Brady. I looked again, but his face was partially covered with blood and I still didn't recognize him. It was as though the horror of his wound had blinded me at first. Then I realized that the bleeding head had a bald spot, and the body was the right girth. My God, I thought, it *is* Brady. I felt sick to my stomach.

By this time a squad car had pulled up and police were hustling the suspect into the back seat. I strained to catch a glimpse of him, but he was completely surrounded by Secret Service agents and uniformed officers. NBC cameraman Sheldon Fielman had been videotaping the entire sequence, however, and I asked him if he'd seen the suspect's face. "Yeah," Fielman said. "He was standing right next to us when he fired. He's young . . . blonde . . . and in his early twenties."

I heard a White House aide shouting, "Get back, get back," in an attempt to clear a path for medics, who had arrived with three ambulances. As they began lifting the three wounded men onto stretchers, I suddenly realized I couldn't wait any longer to phone in a report.

I ran for a telephone to call NBC and dictate my report of the shooting. The drugstore on the ground floor of an office complex across T Street looked like the best bet. But the pay phone in the store was broken and another reporter had beaten me to the manager's phone. I couldn't wait, so I ran out the door leading to the corridor of the office building, which turned out to be a maze of blank doors without a single clue or person to direct me. I felt like Alice in the great hall. As I frantically searched for a door that looked like it might lead to a phone, I tried to outline in my mind the details of the shooting—exactly what I had seen and heard. There was no time, I knew, to compose a script, and I would have to be ready to deliver a report on the spot.

The woman sitting behind a desk facing the first open door I came to looked up, startled by my abruptness.

"I'm a reporter," I said, trying to catch my breath. "I'm covering the shooting across the street. Can I use your phone?"

As she answered yes and pointed to a phone, I reached for the receiver and started dialing the operator. My first call was to the NBC radio news desk in New York, because I knew that radio could get the news out faster than television.

"This is Judy Woodruff," I said. "I'm covering the President and he's just been shot at. We think he's all right. But three people have been hit, including Press Secretary James Brady. I don't have time to do a detailed, blow-by-blow narration of what happened. Ask me some questions."

The radio news editor began firing questions at me. What did you see? Where is the President? What did the suspect look like? How seriously hurt are the wounded? I answered as many of his questions as I could, but I knew that the clock was ticking away and I had yet to call the Washington bureau. "I have to go," I said, cutting him off.

When I phoned the Washington news desk, Les Kretman, the assignment editor, was standing by with bureau chief Sid Davis. They already knew about the shooting, having first heard from an NBC courier, who had been at the hotel to pick up some videotape. I also learned later that ABC radio was on the air with a bulletin four minutes after the shooting. Kretman asked me what I had seen and I reeled off as fast as I could an eyewitness account of the shooting. Then Davis came on the phone and told me that NBC was preparing to begin live, running coverage immediately. "We want you to go live at the White House," he said, "and tell us what you saw."

I dashed out of the office, down the hall, and out to the street to find a cab to drive me back to the White House. Police had set up a barricade between me and Connecticut Avenue, the most direct route to the White House. So I ran in the opposite direction, down T Street to Florida Avenue. My pool crew, whom I had lost in the confusion, suddenly appeared and began running along with me toward Florida Avenue, where we practically commandeered the first approaching taxi.

Within minutes of piling into the cab we heard a report over the taxi radio that the President's limousine had been spotted at George Washington University Hospital. The report speculated that Reagan was at the hospital to check on Brady, who had been taken there along with the wounded Secret Service agent.

That drive took the longest ten minutes I've ever known. The cab reached the White House about 3:05 and dropped us off at the northwest gate, which faces Pennsylvania Avenue. Because my brain was racing—partly from shock, partly to absorb every detail of what had happened in the twenty-five minutes since the shots had been fired—my sense of time was distorted. It seemed like hours had lapsed since the President had ended his speech. In fact, it had been only forty-five minutes.

I ran through the security check at the gate, flashing my press pass at the guards, and sprinted up the drive toward the double doors which open into the briefing room, situated between the White House press office and the press room, where my booth is located. As soon as I entered, I could see that the place was in pandemonium. Press aides and reporters were running back and forth from the press office to the press room, off to the left. I looked for an official who could confirm or deny the radio report that Reagan had been taken to the hospital, and tell me why. But no one in authority was in the office and the subordinate staff didn't know any more than I did.

In the rear of the briefing room I found an NBC crew already set up to go live. Near me were reporters huddled around television sets, trying to learn what had happened. Already, the three networks had suspended regular programming and were on the air live with running accounts of the shooting and reports from correspondents on the scene at George Washington Hospital.

The NBC cameraman who had stayed behind at the White House rushed over to me as soon as I entered the briefing room.

"They want you to go live right away," he said.

"I know, I know," I replied. "Give me a second."

I ran back to the NBC booth in the rear of the press room to collect my thoughts and my IFB, a small earpiece used by reporters in the field during live newscasts to receive instructions from the production people in the studio. Back in the briefing room, my soundman hooked up the IFB and I scrambled up onto a vacant chair, so that the television camera, which is fixed to a tripod on a raised platform in the rear of the room, could get a clear shot of me over the crowd of reporters. Through the IFB I heard the voice of a producer telling me to stand by for Marvin Kalb to ask me a question. Although Kalb usually covers the State Department, he is one of several NBC correspondents who are asked to serve as backup anchors in the Washington studio, in case a news event occurs that warrants broadcast before the next regularly scheduled newscast. Kalb threw it to me, saying, "Tell us what you saw."

More than at any time in my career, I intuitively felt the tremendous responsibility I had to the public and the importance of measuring every word in describing what had happened. My description, I knew, would be the first eyewitness account millions of viewers would hear of the attempt on the President's life. But above all, I sensed it was important to appear calm, so as not to convey an air of panic. Uncertainty about whether the President had been hit and the nation's horror at the wounding of three men were traumatic enough.

Days later, when people asked me how I had managed to appear so unruffled after witnessing the attempted assassination of the President, I couldn't explain it. My calm outward appearance had been a reflexive response more than a calculated one—the culmination of years of experience and training. It was the manner in which any experienced, responsible reporter would have reacted.

Step by step, I recounted everything I had seen and heard from the instant the shots exploded. I described what I had been told by other eyewitnesses, being careful to distinguish between what I knew and what I had heard. I said that although there was speculation that the President had been hit, I could not confirm that. I stressed that other eyewitnesses had said that the President was not hit and that the White House had not confirmed the President's condition.

Then Kalb asked me if I could tell who had done the shooting. I described police wrestling the suspect to the ground within moments of the gunfire and what NBC cameraman Sheldon Fielman had told me the man looked like. Remembering the Secret Service agent I had seen looking up at the roof immediately after the shots rang out, I said I couldn't be sure that the suspect was the only gunman, and that there *might* have been some shooting from overhead. Because of the controversy surrounding the assassination of President Kennedy, I wanted to be especially careful not to jump to any conclusions about who had been doing the shooting and from where.

Despite my good intentions, some assassination conspiracy buffs didn't hesitate to interpret my remarks as evidence that there *were* in fact other gunmen involved in the attack on Reagan. As the evidence developed and it became clear that one man, John Hinckley, acted alone, they weren't dissuaded. I still receive letters from these conspiracy seekers trying to persuade me that other gunmen were involved in the Reagan shooting.

I spent the two hours after my first live report more or less glued to that chair in the briefing room, as I stood by to provide periodic live recaps and to add new facts as they unfolded sporadically throughout the afternoon. My NBC colleagues at the White House, John Palmer and Bill Lynch, did much of the legwork for those White House updates. They shuttled between my chair and the press office to keep me posted so that I, in turn, could provide up-to-the-minute accounts to our viewers. Meanwhile, on a nearby television monitor, I followed NBC correspondents Ken Bode and Chris Wallace, who were standing by at the hospital, where Brady, the wounded Secret Service agent, and the President had been taken.

The scene in the briefing room was crowded and chaotic, with everyone either gathered around television monitors or in the White House press office, attempting to sort out answers in the midst of confusion. The situation was exacerbated by the absence of an authoritative spokesman to whom reporters could turn, including Deputy Press Secretary Larry Speakes, who'd gone to the hospital. With the press secretary lying on the operating table, it was some time before reporters knew whom they could rely upon for information. David Gergen, the White House staff director and, until then, behind the scenes media strategist, tried to reassure reporters, who were frustrated because they were obtaining more information from televised newscasts than from the White House. "Hold on, hold on," Gergen pleaded, "we don't know what has happened yet."

Meanwhile, we learned from television reporters that the White House decision makers—Meese, Deaver, and Baker—were at the hospital and beyond our reach. Their presence there left Administration officials at the White House floundering in the attempt to answer reporters' questions during that first hour after the shooting, and gave credence to the word filtering out of the hospital's emergency room that the President had indeed been wounded and was undergoing surgery.

At about 3:37—more than an hour after the shooting—Gergen stepped to the briefing room podium to verify the President's injury. "Good afternoon," he said. "This is to confirm the statements made at George Washington Hospital that the President was shot once in the left side this afternoon as he left the hotel. His condition is stable. A decision is now being made whether or not to operate to remove the bullet. The White House and the Vice President are in communication. And the Vice President is now en route to Washington." At about the same time, Reagan political adviser Lyn Nofziger was making a similar announcement at the hospital.

For the first time, the thought flashed through my mind that the President might die as a result of the incident I had witnessed.

Gergen's announcement triggered more questions than it dispelled. The delay in confirming Reagan's condition—an honest attempt, I believe, to gather all the facts first—heightened speculation that the condition of the seventy-year-old President was actually much worse than the White House was acknowledging. At the same time, Reagan's incapacitation opened the door to questions about what steps the government

22

was taking to maintain its equilibrium in the immediate aftermath of this national crisis.

As it turned out, the Reagan Administration found itself embarrassingly unprepared to answer those questions and thus reassure the country that things were under control. Probably the most inept effort to provide that needed reassurance from the podium was by Secretary of State Alexander Haig, who later explained he had been frustrated by a statement about a military alert, made by Larry Speakes. I had never seen Haig look so shaken or sound so unsteady. It made me wonder just how serious the President's condition was. "Crisis management is in effect," Haig told the nation and the world in a voice cracking with emotion. "Constitutionally, you have the President, the Vice President, and the Secretary of State in that order. As of now, I am in control here in the White House, pending the return of the Vice President."

As the afternoon wore on, however, the Reagan White House left the distinct impression it didn't know who was in control—while the President underwent surgery to remove a bullet from his left side and Vice President Bush jetted back to Washington aboard Air Force Two from his speech before a group of Texas cattlemen. Deputy Press Secretary Larry Speakes was saying that Defense Secretary Caspar Weinberger was supposed to be third in command in the event of a crisis. A spokesman in the Vice President's office produced yet another answer. The spokesman said he had not heard specifically about anyone's being third after the Vice President.

Against this confusing backdrop, broadcast correspondents were attempting live coverage on the run, trying to piece together developments as they occurred in one of the most competitive news stories ever. The intensity of that competition was demonstrated by the number of broadcast news organizations that claimed "firsts" in reporting the attack on the President. ABC radio was first to broadcast a bulletin at

2:30, supplied by ABC television's White House correspondent Sam Donaldson, who was at the scene. Cable News Network, which did not have a camera on the scene of the shooting, nevertheless claimed to have provided the first television report with a bulletin at 2:33. Walt Rogers of AP radio said he was first on the air with audio of the gunshots at 2:33. ABC television, which had a camera at the scene, was on the air with its bulletin at 2:34 and broadcast the first, rough, unedited piece of videotape of the attack eight minutes later. NBC and CBS ran bulletins at 2:38, with videotape on CBS at 2:46, and NBC at 2:47. As NBC's reporter on the scene, I felt partly responsible for our not being first.

But sadly, that pressure to be first led to the major error committed by all three networks, as well as one of the wire services, in reporting that James Brady had died from the head wound he had suffered. The erroneous report illustrated how broadcasting unconfirmed reports in the effort to be first in providing up-to-the-minute news can snowball dangerously.

The first report of Brady's death was aired by CBS, which claimed Senate Majority Leader Howard Baker's office as its source. ABC, which picked up the story from CBS, then claimed confirmation by White House Assistant Press Secretary David Prosperi. But Prosperi said later that the over-eager ABC reporter had misunderstood him. Together with John Palmer and Bill Lynch, I kept trying to confirm the other networks' reports through White House sources, but to no avail. Despite that—after a report of Brady's death by one of the wire services—NBC also went on the air with it.

I had already left my "live" position on the briefing-room chair and gone back to the NBC booth to begin preparing a story for the evening newscast when I heard from the TV monitor that the Brady reports were false. A spokesman at the hospital assured the assembled press that Brady, though in critical condition, was alive. What a welcome piece of news, I thought. But then the image of his wife, Sarah, whom I knew and liked, flashed through my mind. I was suddenly full of regret that such a glaring error had been made by so many. Unfortunately, this wasn't the only mistake we made that tension-filled day: NBC erroneously reported that Reagan had undergone open-heart surgery. These incidents were a painful reminder for all of us in the news business that the pressure to be first must always take a back seat to our obligation to be accurate.

This rainy Monday, which had begun in such an ordinary fashion, provided another equally significant lesson: the importance of vigilant news coverage of the president. Within a matter of heartbeats, a routine public appearance had become the most urgent and crucial news story in the nation and the world—it took John Hinckley just 1-2 seconds to squeeze off six shots. The absolute need to cover the President's every step, to keep an eye on him at all times, and to appreciate the function of the Secret Service, which reporters often consider a nuisance, were all shockingly underscored by the series of chilling instant replays of the attempted assassination broadcast throughout the afternoon by all three networks.

With a half-dozen network television cameras rolling, the shooting outside the Hilton was undoubtedly the most extensively covered assassination attempt in history. More important, it was the most thoroughly documented. NBC cameraman Sheldon Fielman, who had started his camera outside the hotel when Secret Service agents indicated that the President was on his way, locked onto Reagan as soon as he emerged through the VIP door, and held the picture as he heard the shots. After the President was shot, Fielman turned to his right, opened the zoom lens, and caught John Hinckley's hand holding a gun within inches of the camera. He kept rolling until Hinckley was driven away by police.

When I reached home a little after midnight, the day's events had only begun to sink in. My husband, Al, met me in the downstairs hallway and hugged me, just as I was about to collapse into a chair. My body was bone-tired, but my brain was still racing, churning over what had happened. It was as if I'd been receiving an extra dose of adrenalin every hour on the hour since the shooting. Now, I felt drained.

For twenty minutes or so, Al and I talked—or rather I talked and he listened. As I sat there reflecting on what a searing day it had been, I thought about how vulnerable a president is. And I thought about how, if I had it all to do over again, God forbid, I would stand closer to the President and get to the phone faster.

I felt so sad for Jim Brady's wife, Sarah, and for the families of everyone who had been wounded. I felt sad, too, for the whole country. What kind of world is this that my baby would soon be born into? I wondered. Why do these senseless acts of violence against our leaders keep being repeated?

It was so depressing and so frightening to think about. I kept saying to Al, over and over again, that I couldn't believe what had happened. He confided his own fear that day. When he first heard that the President had been shot at and three others had been wounded, his first thought was that I was in the travel pool. He ran to a television set to find out who the injured were, terrified that I might be one of them. Five or ten awful minutes passed before he learned I was safe.

Silently, we climbed the stairs to the bedroom.

Cue the White House

Whenever someone describes my job as glamorous, I smile and tell them about the lunches of Lance crackers; the sunrise "stand-ups" in subzero weather on the White House lawn for the "Today" show; the two- and three-hour "stakeouts," consisting of nothing but waiting for a potential newsmaker to emerge; the ten-hour days; and the news that breaks minutes before deadline. Somehow, then, it doesn't seem quite so glamorous.

It's not that I'm complaining, though I do my fair share of that. I continue to find the White House assignment a very rewarding one. The visibility is enormous. And walking through the black wrought iron gates at 1600 Pennsylvania Avenue to go to work beats punching the time clock at the Atlanta printing firm where I used to set type part-time to supplement my first television salary. Moreover, the job has its glittering moments. In my five years on the White House beat I have traveled with the President to twenty-one countries on five continents; at home, I've been in well over half the states and enjoyed such wonders as the Salmon River in Idaho (when Jimmy Carter vacationed there in the summer of 1978). I've met world leaders and interviewed cabinet members, senators, congressmen, and other dignitaries who came to call on the President.

My job also brings me a measure of recognition. Strangers

sometimes stop me on the street or in airports and ask, "Aren't you Lesley Stahl?" "No," I tell them straight-faced, "I'm Sam Donaldson." It still surprises me that my views on the White House and president-press relations are sometimes sought by political experts, authors, civic groups, and university professors.

The most important entree, however, is the special vantage I enjoy from which to observe the man who helps shape the destiny of millions of lives and might profoundly affect the course of history. As the late Philip Graham, publisher of the *Washington Post* said, we journalists provide the "first rough draft" of history. And trying to understand and report on how a president is handling his awesome responsibilities and wielding power is the real glamour of my job.

Nevertheless, covering the White House for a television network is not what many people seem to imagine—reading presidential pronouncements before the television camera while standing knee-deep in stardust and status. Mostly, it's a lot of hard work. Anyone who comes to the job thinking otherwise will quickly find herself standing knee-deep in something other than stardust.

It also has more than its share of trivia. Every President has several appointments a week of such earth-shattering importance as a visit from South Carolina Senator Strom Thurmond and Mrs. America. And holidays seem to bring out the best in White House silliness: During one Thanksgiving in the Carter Administration, a wild turkey was loose for two days on the White House grounds. And another Thanksgiving saw reporters eagerly thrusting their microphones forward to catch a conversation between President-elect Reagan and a noisy gobbler.

It's also fiercely competitive. There are only a handful of television networks and we are on the air at about the same time every night during the week. Not only is the competition intense among this small group, but the results are immediately apparent to millions of viewers. With considerable stakes involved, every night I find myself up against men and women for whom I have tremendous professional respect. And I happen to like very much people such as Sam Donaldson and Ann Compton of ABC and Bill Plante and Lesley Stahl of CBS. I also want to put a better product on the air than they do.

Further, the job has more than its share of frustrations. Countless hours are spent chasing false leads, or searching for bits of information to fill out a story, or merely waiting for something to happen. This frustration is endemic to the beat.

I am usually up before seven each day to watch the morning news programs—chiefly NBC's "Today" show, but switching to ABC and CBS during breaks—and to read the morning paper for clues to stories I might want to develop. Although there is no such thing as a "normal" day covering the White House, February 12, 1981, probably is as typical as any. Today there is a story in the *Washington Post* about a disagreement between the President's economic advisers over how optimistic the upcoming economic forecast should be. It's an interesting topic—one which I have spent some time reporting—but I'm not sure it can be turned into an easily understood television piece. Also, this is John Palmer's day (he is my NBC colleague covering the White House) to prepare a piece for the evening news, so I must try to pick up other threads.

After lunch with a White House staffer, I start pursuing other story possibilities, but there is a last-minute surprise. A loudspeaker in the press area announces that the Italian foreign minister, who has been in for a short meeting with Reagan, will be available in front of the West Wing lobby. I rush to pull a camera crew off its lunch break, literally in mid-hamburger, to cover the ambassador and Secretary of State Haig. But the frenzy is for naught. As in so many of these impromptu interviews, there is no news.

I spend the rest of the day gearing up for the evening, but not for fun. Tonight it is my turn to work, and it is also NBC's turn to be travel pool. The assignment is the Reagans' dinner at the Vice President's house. At about 6:45 ten members of the press pool are escorted out to the south grounds of the White House to sit in two vans and await the departure of the Reagans. We are part of a motorcade that includes the presidential limousine. But the thrill of that ends at the Bushes' curbside. The NBC camera crew in the first van opens up the sunroof to take pictures of the limousine pulling onto the grounds. But only the Reagan limousine and a single Secret Service follow-up car are permitted to enter the driveway. That's when the reporters tear out of vans and race up to the house. I run up as the Bushes and Reagans are disappearing inside and do not get close enough to ask a question. While the President enjoys his dinner, the reporters and crew are driven to a nearby restaurant, returning just before nine. About thirty minutes later, reporters shout a question at Reagan as he emerges from the house. It is about the budget. He answers, but tries to keep it light and short, saying, "It's cold." We dash back to the vans: The President's limousine waits for no one. These events I would just as soon miss. All this star-chasing and, once again, no news.

But the headline-making days are what really keeps us limber. That's when the frantic scramble for telling quotes, sharp photos, and the best angle on the story starts reporters on a relay race through Washington's back rooms and front stages. These days begin in our own back room, the press house.

All day, reporters from competing networks are forced to huddle close by, though not together. Our NBC booth fills one corner of the back of the press room in the West Wing of the White House. The booth, which measures eight feet by six feet, is like a deep closet with two windows overlooking the press room. Our sliding door is slammed back and forth many times each day. I share this very limited space with my colleagues John Palmer and Andrea Mitchell and a seven-foot-long counter with three typewriters and three chairs that were somehow squeezed in. Immediately adjacent is an even smaller sound-proof booth where radio spots and "voice over" television spots are narrated. What makes these clam-shell environs clammier still is the nerve-wracking QWIP machine. A monster of modernism, the QWIP is constantly fed pieces of typed paper, which it transmits noisily to the "Nightly News" production offices in Washington or the radio headquarters. Editors stand by to clear our scripts for later telecast.

The CBS and ABC booths, which are almost identical to ours in size and shape, are next to us. And every night at six-thirty or seven, the dials on the television sets in all three booths are switched, not only to catch our own pieces but to see what the competition did. In our separate huddles, there is much mental note-taking going on.

In this atmosphere it is understandably a heady sensation to beat the competition. A day before President Reagan unveiled his first budget, I reported that the deficit would be $45 billion, or about $17 billion more than the supposedly bigger-spending Carter Administration proposed. In the context, this was a nice piece of irony, all the more so since ABC mistakenly reported on the same night that the proposed Reagan budget deficit would be only $17.5 billion. I assured my producers we were right—though I suspect some kept their fingers crossed for the next twenty-four hours.

More important, though, than such transitory "scoops," are judgment calls. In 1979, President Carter was engaging in some shuttle diplomacy in the Middle East, trying to expedite the Camp David peace process. After several days in Jerusalem, top Carter aides seemed to suggest that the President's efforts were failing due to Israeli intransigence. Knowing the penchant of some Carter aides to poor-mouth prospects—a trait dating back to Carter's political campaigns—and having at least one reliable source who was certain a solution was imminent, I didn't take the bait. As a result, NBC was the only network that didn't strongly suggest the talks were falling apart. An agreement was reached the next day. A few days later, I received a very sweet thank-you telegram from John Chancellor.

Of course, if those days produce great highs, we know the lows will come too. There have been more evenings than I care to remember when I felt that my longtime competitor, Sam Donaldson, drove home a pertinent point or used a pungent line that I wished I'd thought of. This problem isn't limited to ABC, unfortunately. In the summer of 1981 my heart sank one night as I watched CBS's Bill Plante scoop the rest of us on the U.S.'s decision to delay shipping sophisticated jet fighters to Israel. A few months earlier, I was leisurely watching the "CBS Evening News" when Lesley Stahl suddenly appeared on the air saying the Reagan Administration was about to lift the Soviet grain embargo. Both times, I braced for the inevitable call from NBC asking why we didn't have the story. The answer was simple: we were beaten.

One of the few times this competition took on a personally unpleasant air was in November 1979. After numerous phone calls, I had learned that President Carter was about to appoint federal judge Shirley Hufstedler to be Secretary of the new Department of Education. I went to the White House lawn a little after six P.M. to do what would be an exclusive report on this nomination. My colleague Lesley Stahl was standing nearby, having just finished another story. She stayed there, and as I began my piece she heard my report. She then went inside to call CBS, and, based on her information, they reported that evening on the imminent Hufstedler appointment. To make matters even worse, CBS had it on the air a few minutes before we did. The next day Lesley was apologetic, explaining that once she heard my report, she felt obligated to inform her network. I think we both realized she had made a mistake, that the incident was an aberration.

One place that none of us ever gets a scoop—or much information, for that matter—is at the daily skirmish called the White House press briefing. The word briefing is a misnomer; it is actually a war of wills between the briefer, the presidential press secretary, who wants to give us information that suits the purposes of the White House, and the press, who always want more than they are told and usually more than there is to tell. These sessions take place in the press room located off the walkway between the West Wing of the White House and the residence. Generally, they are scheduled to start at about noon each day. In the Carter Administration, Press Secretary Jody Powell was notoriously late, and the briefings often didn't start until mid-afternoon. In the Reagan Administration, Deputy Press Secretary Larry Speakes takes pride in punctuality and seldom starts even minutes late. David Gergen, Reagan's communications director, falls somewhere between these two extremes.

Usually there are four or five dozen reporters present, many of whom, after the press secretary's perfunctory opening statements announcing schedules or presidential meetings, begin by shouting questions. These "briefings" can last anywhere from twenty minutes to two hours. Unfortunately, they are often dominated by the louder members of the press corps. But some of our wittier colleagues entertain us with one-liners and *sotto voce* comments that discourage any of us from taking ourselves too seriously. For instance, Sam Donaldson brought one restless Friday briefing to a halt after he asked Larry

Speakes if the President believed so many people were out of work because the unemployment rate was so high.

As news gathering sessions, these briefings tend to be disappointing, yet it's probably healthy that the White House has to prepare for them each day. Moreover, sometimes they're the source of hints of stories that may be pursued, productively, later. For example, when the briefer responds to a question with, "I have nothing for you on that," it usually means the reporter is on the right track, and a few properly placed phone calls should bring confirmation.

One day in early 1982 Larry Speakes opened a briefing by bringing on a Mississippi folk singer who, strumming his guitar, sang a blues number about the White House press corps. Jody Powell would sometimes regale us with his folksy, Southern stories about slugs, grasshoppers, frogs, and the like. But these exchanges can also deteriorate into bitter encounters between the podium and the press; an air of mistrust, even hostility, dates back to the Watergate era.

From my viewpoint, it is especially frustrating that the White House frequently manipulates the timing of news, putting it out late in the day so that we not only have a physically exhausting, mind-boggling task, but precious little time to think about sharp analysis or to do independent reporting. Naturally, this occurs much more often when the news is embarrassing to the White House. The briefing to announce the departure of Reagan's national security adviser, Richard Allen, started at 5:35 P.M. I led the "NBC Nightly News" less than an hour later, and my closing comments were live from the White House's north lawn. It wasn't any better during the Carter years. Once when the White House had to disclose that the President had sent cables to U.S. diplomats in Libya in advance of one of his brother's controversial trips there, they made the announcement on a Friday night shortly after seven—just in time to miss the networks' news broadcasts for the week. White House excuses—that it takes time to gather all the necessary information on a story or that announcements that might affect the financial markets have to wait until the stock exchange closes—are usually intended to prevent us from adding perspective to a story that might not put the Administration in the most favorable light.

Even the so-called photo opportunities designed to show the President at work and the steady stream of press releases on every conceivable White House statement, action, or appointment are part of the image-making operation, which is directed by the press office. Interviews with the President on his way to a helicopter are often cut short with a signal to the pilot to rev up the motor.

In presenting the Administration's point of view, the President's image makers leave no detail overlooked. When the President delivers a speech outdoors, his aides make sure that the podium is positioned so that the sun's harsh glare does not accentuate the age lines in his face. And when a group of mayors visits the Oval Office the day after the President has announced cutbacks in federal aid to cities, the White House press office handpicks those who will meet the press afterwards, thus ensuring that any quoted remarks will be as favorable to the President as possible.

Pulling on the other side of the rope is the White House press corps. My job as a reporter is to present the most accurate view of the President—age lines and all—and of his policies and decisions. I am expected to cover those "photo opportunities" and briefings because the President's every action is potentially news. But that does not mean merely reporting what the President or his spokesmen say. I am also expected to interpret the President's actions, decisions, and policies—and that means pursuing views other than the Administration's, including views which may be at odds with the President's.

This tug-of-war between White House image making and the task of news gathering makes covering the President one of the most frustrating and rewarding assignments in daily journalism. And while that may seem to be a contradictory statement, contradictions are a large part of what this job is about.

Take my access to the President, for example. Of all the special doors my job opens to me, the doors to the President and his top aides are, ironically, the most closely guarded. The first rule of the tug-of-war news game is that the Administration always controls access to the President and his men. In practice, this means that reporters' opportunities to see the President or to ask him a question about a news development or an upcoming decision are usually limited to one or two minutes during a photo opportunity. Typically, we are herded into the Oval Office by a White House press aide, with everyone pushing to the front of the pack to try to get the best position from which to photograph the President or ask him a question. As strobe lights flash and television cameras roll, the President and whomever he happens to be meeting with pose for the cameras while making awkward small talk and trying to pretend we're flies on the wall. Occasionally the President will acknowledge the reporters' presence with a word to us, or by briefly answering a question or two. Figuring out the best way to phrase those questions in order to elicit an answer is something I give a lot of thought to. Sometimes framing the question as a challenge is the best tactic; other times asking the President to explain why or how he reached a decision is more effective. Often, when we are on the verge of eliciting a newsworthy comment from him, reporters' questions will prompt the White House press office aide, who is always present for these encounters, to bark, "Lights, please!" to the television crews. That's our cue to stop our picture-taking immediately, thank the President, and shuffle out. So much for chatting with the chief executive.

Most days we are shepherded from one such "news event" to the next by the press secretary or one of his staff. One day it may be an award ceremony in the Rose Garden during which the President presents a group of teenagers with the Young American Medal for Bravery and Freedom. Another day it may be the arrival of South Korean President Chun to pay a state visit. On that occasion—not at all atypical—we waited fifteen minutes in the rain in order to see President Reagan and Vice President Bush greet Chun as he stepped out of his limousine into the White House driveway. The dignitaries, of course, were sheltered by a canopy. No words were spoken, just brief posing for photographers and television cameras.

Even though it's rare that any news emerges from these carefully orchestrated events, or that they ever appear on the air as stories, I must attend them in case something unexpected, and therefore newsworthy, does occur. Chasing these false alarms in hopes of finding a fire takes up a large part of my day. But I am less frustrated by such seemingly fruitless adventures than I was during my first months of covering the White House, because I have learned that missing a photo opportunity may mean missing some gesture or facial expression, or not knowing which White House aides were involved. Such details may enhance my story for the day or transform an essentially routine event into news. When the President's eyes fill with tears as he delivers an emotional speech, or when he drops his note cards and flubs his remarks, or when he stops to answer a reporter's question as he strides across the South Lawn toward a waiting helicopter—that's news. And while a print reporter can reconstruct the scene or the President's statement later if he misses something newsworthy, I must be there to make sure that my crew gets it on camera. In television news, if you don't have the pictures, you often don't have the story, though with improved creative technology, this isn't as absolute as it used to be.

Still, the amount of time we must spend covering the President during stage-managed events on the off chance that something newsworthy may occur often makes us chafe. And nobody chafes more than ABC's Sam Donaldson, the Peck's bad boy of the White House press corps. A tough reporter when he is onto a story, Donaldson tends to become impatient when he is stuck covering one of those questionably newsworthy Rose Garden award ceremonies. His whispered wisecracks and sardonic outbursts are all the more humorous because Donaldson usually gets away with them. One time he did not, however, was during the arrival ceremony for British Prime Minister Margaret Thatcher. Thatcher's limousine pulled up amid all the pomp and circumstance that the White House could muster. An assemblage which included the President & Mrs. Reagan, the diplomatic corps, the White House staff, Cabinet members, the honor guards from each branch of the military, a crowd of several hundred, and, of course, the White House press corps, stood at the North Portico entrance, waiting for the British Prime Minister to emerge from her car. Several long, silent seconds lapsed until, suddenly, Donaldson's voice boomed, "Bring her on!" If looks could kill, today Donaldson would be doing his stand-ups in front of the pearly gates instead of the White House after the glare presidential counselor Ed Meese gave him. We heard later that Meese had an aide call ABC executives to warn that unless Donaldson restrained himself and his irreverence, his press pass would be revoked.

On the rare occasion when the White House grants an interview with the President, it is usually to a group of editors or a news anchor instead of the regular White House reporter. White House image makers determine when to permit a presidential interview and, by deciding which interview requests will be accepted, indirectly decide who will conduct it. They know that giving presidential interviews to the established political columnists and network news anchors helps ensure that the President's answers will receive maximum coverage, either on the newspaper's front page or during the network's evening newscast. For those of us who cover the President daily, our limited opportunities to question him are one more frustrating example of the tug-of-war over control of White House news.

During five years of covering the White House, I have participated in one formal presidential interview—with Ronald Reagan, one month after his inauguration and on the afternoon before his first major address on the economy. The ground rules were carefully outlined by the White House in advance: the interview would last forty minutes and no television cameras would be permitted. At 3:30 that February afternoon, Lesley Stahl of CBS, Sam Donaldson of ABC, and I were ushered into the map room on the first floor of the White House mansion by Press Secretary James Brady, who gestured to us to take our seats in the four armchairs arranged in a semicircle before the lit fireplace. Partly because of the time limitation, partly because I wanted to be well prepared for my first presidential interview, I had stayed up late the night before, studying Reaganomics and drawing up a list of questions. I knew that the White House saw the interview as a promotion for the President's prime-time speech, figuring that the evening news reports by the White House correspondents would serve to remind viewers to tune in later. This was our chance, though, to ask the President some questions about the divergent philosophies behind Reaganomics. On the one hand, he was advocating expensive supply-side tax cuts and military spending programs in the face of growing government deficits; on the other, he was supporting tighter controls on the growth of money through higher interest rates. Some economists were worried that trying to reconcile these two divergent views could bring about the worst possible combination of big deficits and high interest rates.

Reagan entered the map room, smiling, took the fourth

chair next to the fireplace, and began the interview in his best, aw-shucks-I'm-just-an-old-horse-cavalry-man manner by apologizing to Lesley Stahl and me for having called us "young ladies" during a press conference earlier in the week. He said he was still having a difficult time remembering all the reporters names and he hoped we would forgive him for forgetting ours. I was completely disarmed. We hadn't even begun the interview and already the President had shrewdly set the tone of the meeting as that of a friendly fireside chat—not the sort of mood you are eager to disrupt by challenging him with a question like, "How can you cut taxes and increase defense spending at the same time and hope to achieve a balanced budget?" I was beginning to understand why Ronald Reagan was scoring such high marks for persuasiveness.

Although I came away from that interview feeling that Reagan truly believed his economic program would work, I didn't have any clearer sense of how he planned to make it work. I never really got a full shot at my question, however. That was due mostly to time constraints and to the fact that I wasn't more forceful. Even so, I did acquire a good lesson in the vaunted Reagan charm.

But if presidents and presidential advisers can be charming, they can also be critical and even ruthless. The White House rarely hesitates to let reporters know when they disagree with coverage or interpretation of an event. Curtis Wilkie of the *Boston Globe,* one of the more talented as well as colorful White House correspondents, used to complain that the Carter White House deliberately excluded him from important background briefings as punishment for his tough pieces on the President. My husband is convinced that the Carterites did the same to the *Wall Street Journal.* This sort of response isn't a partisan phenomenon. The Reagan Administration threatened to cancel a longstanding prime-time interview with Roger Mudd of NBC because they were so displeased with the anchorman's stinging critique of Reagan's performance during a December 1981 news conference. Mudd scored the President for not knowing about an important Supreme Court civil rights decision, among other shortcomings. The White House was furious about Mudd's report, which was actually very fair: Even Reagan aides were dismayed by his performance.

I have received my share of complaining calls from White House officials who didn't agree with a piece they thought was too critical. Once during the Carter presidency, the President didn't call on me at a news conference because, I felt, he was displeased with some of my recent reports. Only in the rarest of circumstances would they expect you to retract what you've reported, but they hope their show of displeasure will affect your next report. It's analogous to baseball players arguing with the umpire. Maybe this tactic works over the short run, but I doubt that it makes much difference over the long haul.

Mail from viewers has little more effect on the way I do my job, but it reminds me again and again how much people apparently hear what they want to hear. After four years of covering the Carter Administration and being accused by viewers of everything from sickening sympathy for Carter to outright hatred of him, the mail on my coverage of the Reagan Administration was equally contradictory.

The critical letters are the most fun to read: A woman in Buffalo asked why I hated President Reagan so much that I would say anything "to embarrass him and make him look incompetent. What has he ever done to you?" Another woman in Austin, Texas, wrote to NBC in New York to complain of my coverage of a news conference: I "did not tell it as he said it," she insisted, adding, "More than that, she looks as though she has just gotten out of bed."

But the Austin letter ended on a note of sympathy: "If she is ill, I'm sorry I said this." Another viewer took great delight when she learned I had had a baby: she sent me a free sample of something called a TempyTug, which she had designed, and described it as a "unique bath water thermometer." The flattering letters are often simple requests for a picture or an autograph, but one of my favorites (from a man who enclosed a picture of me, appearing on his television set) informed me that I was slowly working my way into the lot of women that he most admired in life. "You're up there," he wrote, "along with Liv Ullman, Shirley Chisholm, Ellen Goodman, and Millicent Fenwick."

There are some moments of glamour at the White House, I confess. Although we don't socialize with the President or his top lieutenants very often—nor should we—there are those rare occasions, and they are infrequent enough so that we don't have to worry about compromising ourselves.

One such time occurred in the summer of 1981. The crisp, cream-colored invitation embossed with a gold presidential seal arrived in the mail in a matching envelope hand-addressed to "Mr. and Mrs. Albert Hunt." In engraved lettering it read: "The President and Mrs. Reagan invite you to a State dinner in honor of his Excellency the President of the Arab Republic of Egypt and Mrs. Sadat to be held at the White House on August 5, 1981 at 7:30." The invitation was unexpected. Although I regularly cover White House state dinners, I am not regularly invited to them. I had attended only one other state dinner as a guest: in 1977 in the very early days of the Carter Administration.

I am also not regularly addressed by my husband's name. Whenever I hear someone say, "Mrs. Hunt," I start looking around for my mother-in-law. When I married I kept the name Woodruff because it was sensible to keep it, not because of any feminist conviction. Reporting and television are among the few fields in which your name is stamped on your work, and I thought changing my name would confuse sources and viewers. Credibility and recognizability are a television reporter's most prized possessions, and both hinge to a large extent on the name you have made for yourself through your work. But Washington formal society is bound by a rigid protocol which normally regards all women as the wives of their husbands when it comes to forms of address. Although I am the White House correspondent in the family, as far as protocol is concerned I am Mrs. Albert Hunt.

I phoned the office of the White House social secretary and told her that we were delighted to accept, marked the date on my calendar, and wondered what I would wear.

To the socially striving and politically ambitious, White House invitations are highly coveted. And even the most determined political opponents, as well as those who profess the most cynical nonchalance, are often the most eager to accept. One top television network correspondent told me that he would never accept an invitation to the White House because he thought it would compromise him in writing about the Administration. Then he received one of those "compromising" invitations. "It took me about a minute," he said, "to decide to go."

Evenings at the White House are traditionally marked by a dazzling elegance and a regal sense of decorum. Starchly uniformed military social aides usher guests from one softly lit, antique- and flower-filled room to the next. Presidents and first ladies long since passed into history smile down from gilt-framed portraits. And the high-ranking, important, and merely famous gather to make polite conversation against a backdrop of flickering candles, strolling musicians, gleaming silver, and sumptuous food.

To a President, however, a state dinner is less a social event and more a working expense-account dinner. The tab is picked up by the American taxpayer—from the flowers to the salary of the White House staffer who oversees the selection of bouquets and the seating arrangements. These evenings are as much a part of a President's job as signing bills and holding Cabinet meetings. They are also an intrinsic part of the diplomatic process. In forging friendships with foreign leaders and the countries they represent, state dinners can be just as important as business meetings. For that reason, they are regarded as news and covered by the media, although sometimes the most newsworthy aspect of the evening is who was invited and why. The day I covered a state luncheon for Mexican President Lopez Portillo during the summer of 1981 one of the guests was Fernando Valenzuela, the rookie sensation of the Los Angeles Dodgers. "Find out when he thinks the baseball strike will end," my editor ordered.

When I'm covering a state luncheon or dinner, my deadlines, coupled with the restrictions on access to guests and the rooms in which they gather, mean I am afforded only a superficial glimpse of the affair. Attending a state dinner as a guest, however, provides an opportunity for a firsthand look at how the President performs in his role as First Host to world leaders.

Some Presidents and their wives are better than others in transforming what could easily be a stuffy, albeit glittering, event into an enchanting evening that becomes the talk of the town. And those Presidents who succeed at them find that White House galas can be one of the most effective public relations tools available to them. John Kennedy, for example, mingled "beautiful people" with social-register aristocrats during White House dinners replete with French champagne and Parisian gowns. Besides setting new standards for style and grace at the White House, those celebrated Kennedy dinner parties diverted attention from the New Frontier's failures in dealing with Congress and handling foreign policy.

State dinners under the Carters, on the other hand, were best known as dry affairs in terms both of the tenor of the evening and the absence of hard liquor. Their critics sneered at such teetotaling as yet another example of the Carters' lack of sophistication. Although I think the Carters were unfairly branded as rubes by Washington's social lions, Jimmy and Rosalyn were probably happier hosting casual barbecues on the White House South Lawn than formal dinners in the State dining room.

Unlike the small-town Carters and their grass-roots friends, the Reagans came to Washington equipped with movie-star and business-mogul pals. The moneyed taste and Hollywood glamour of the guests who flocked to White House dinners hosted by the Reagans rapidly established this Administration's reputation for elegance at the White House.

The morning of the dinner, I brought a long dress to work with me. I knew I would be lucky to finish my "Nightly News" piece by the arrival of Anwar Sadat an hour before dinner, and there would be no time to go home to change. I dressed in the ladies lavatory off the press room and walked outside into the muggy August evening to meet Al at the White House gate on Pennsylvania Avenue.

Every step of a State dinner is carefully planned, beginning with the arrival of the guest of honor at the front door of the White House, where he is greeted by the President and First Lady in a red-carpet welcome that includes bayonet-bearing military guards standing at attention. The dignitaries then retire to the private quarters on the third floor to await the other guests.

We arrived at the diplomatic entrance with the other guests, where we were greeted by one of the several military social aides, dressed in white gloves and brass-buttoned uniforms, who hover politely over guests throughout the evening. The aides are there to assure you that, yes, you may sit on the furniture, to answer questions about White House decor, and to make sure that you are never alone in a corner. Our aide gave each of us a card with our seat assignment for dinner and led us out to the Cross Hall. There, reporters who were covering the dinner stood behind red velvet ropes, noted the arrival of guests whose names were formally announced as they passed by, and shouted questions at the more recognizable ones in hopes of prompting some interesting quotes for their stories. I felt embarrassed having my name announced to other reporters with whom I would normally be standing. But Elizabeth Bumiller, a friend with the *Washington Post,* broke the ice by shouting to us, as though we were potential news items, "Hey, when are you going to have the baby?" With joking self-importance, Al replied, "I'll have a press availability later," as we were escorted past her and up the marble staircase to the East Room.

The East Room is the largest and probably the most historic reception room in the White House. It was here that the body of John Kennedy lay in state and Richard Nixon bade a tearful farewell to his aides before resigning from office. And it was here that Pablo Casals played, Beverly Sills sang, and Mikhail Baryshnikov danced. Tonight it was the room where guests were officially announced to the rest of the party and mingled over drinks before dinner, while a military ensemble played softly in the Great Hall.

It's a heady feeling to be standing there sipping drinks as a dinner guest at the White House. The side of the mansion that tourists see during the day may seem cold and lacking in heart. But at night, with the dimmed lights, ubiquitous flowers, and soft music filtering through the air, those same formal public rooms seem warm and romantic.

As I glanced around the East Room, I could see the awe on the faces of many of the guests—Democrats and Republicans, corporate heads and prominent socialites. They had read about those historic White House dinners where Thomas Jefferson had introduced such foreign dishes as macaroni; Dolley Madison had reigned; and the New Deal, the New

Frontier, and the Great Society had entertained in fine style. Now they were here, rubbing shoulders with the names in the news: Vice President George Bush, Senate Majority Leader Howard Baker, Secretary of State Alexander Haig, and celebrity statesman Henry Kissinger. And as if these news celebrities weren't glamorous enough, several movie stars were there to round out the scenery: Omar "Dr. Zhivago" Sharif, Roger "007" Moore, and Robert "Untouchable" Stack.

Several of the guests looked scared to death, as though worried about making some terrible gaffe like spilling their drinks on the antique rugs. Others merely looked uncertain, as though they might be wondering whether it was all right to walk up to Kissinger or Bush and introduce themselves. And still others appeared completely self-satisfied, secure in the knowledge that they were here tonight because they *counted.*

Precisely at 7:30, the band struck up "Ruffles and Flourishes," followed by "Hail to the Chief." While guests continued to mingle in the East Room, the President and Mrs. Reagan made their grand entrance with the Sadats down the marble staircase, preceded by four military guards bearing flags. At the bottom of the stairs, an aide announced the dignitaries, who posed briefly for photographers and television crews, while society and fashion reporters noted that Nancy Reagan wore a white Albert Nippon dress with puffed sleeves and a full skirt and Jehan Sadat wore a pale blue chiffon dress. Although State dinners are normally black-tie affairs, the men wore dark business suits this night.

The President and his party formed the receiving line as soon as they entered the East Room. For most of the 100 guests, this would be the only opportunity, however brief, to speak with the dignitaries all evening. The task for the President and his wife is to make each "Nice to see you" sound genuine and personable, while military aides gently nudge

guests to keep the line moving smoothly. Although I imagine
that it's a real test after the first ten handshakes, the Reagans
managed to come across graciously.

As I was introduced to President Sadat, I was struck by
how weary he looked. I had last seen him face-to-face two
years before, when I accompanied Jimmy Carter to Egypt
during the Middle East peace talks there, and I had been
impressed then by Sadat's easy smile and determined optimism.
Now he had come to call on another American President,
hoping to establish the same friendship he had shared with
Jimmy Carter. With him Sadat had brought a long list of
requests which he considered crucial to the peace process, and
most of which the Reagan Administration was not prepared
to fill.

This Washington visit was to be Sadat's last. Nine weeks
later, he was gunned down near Cairo by some of his own
soldiers as he reviewed a military parade.

Except for the Reagans and the Sadats, couples were seated
at separate tables in the gold-and-white candlelit state dining
room. I was flanked by pianist Robert Fizdale and British
actor Roger Moore, also known as James Bond, the fictional
playboy super-spy Moore has played in several films. As the
Marine Corps strolling strings played and we dined on cold
Columbia River salmon with sauce verte, supreme of Royal
Squab veronique, wild rice, green beans, salad, Port Salut
cheese, and fresh peach mousse Cardinal with almond tuilies,
socialite Mrs. C. Z. Guest surveyed the scene and pronounced
it "so soigne." She told a society reporter that night, "All
the flowers, the plants, the perfect taste! I'll tell my friends
when I go back to Saratoga that I sat between Roger
Moore and Mr. [Michael] Deaver." With all due respect to
Michael Deaver, Reagan's deputy chief of staff, I told my
friends about sitting with Roger Moore. He was deeply tanned
and handsome, with an easy, self-effacing sense of humor

which prompted him to crack, when asked why he had been invited, "Maybe because I filmed in Egypt. And I'm *very* good on a camel."

Dinner ended at about nine-thirty with the traditional exchange of toasts between the President and the guest of honor—the one time during such evenings when remarks usually shift from convivial to serious. Sadat's toast was a prod to the President to begin a dialogue with the Palestine Liberation Organization. "It would be an act of statesmanship and vision," the Egyptian leader said, as Reagan smiled noncommitally. I found myself automatically thinking that Sadat's toast was the lead for tonight's story, even though I wasn't supposed to be working.

Afterwards, we moved back to the East Room for coffee and entertainment, a piano duet of classical selections, followed by after-dinner drinks in the Blue Room and dancing and champagne in the Great Hall. By now, it was more than just history and glamour that was making the guests feel heady. At about eleven-thirty, the Reagans signaled the end of the evening by retiring upstairs. We and the other guests left a few minutes later, reluctantly but not wanting to overstay our welcome.

As Al and I drove home in our 1980 Dodge Omni, I felt a little like Cinderella after her coach had turned into a pumpkin.

The dinner for Anwar Sadat was a rare inside look for this White House correspondent. Instead of soft music and candlelight, my evenings at the executive mansion are often dominated by a race against the clock to meet my deadline for the radio report I must file—a network feed to NBC affiliates around the country for use during their 11 P.M. newscasts. Instead of being ushered by a white-gloved military aide from one softly lit, elegantly furnished stateroom to the next, I sprint back and forth from the press room to designated photo opportunities which are announced Big Brother style over the loudspeaker in the press room: "Everyone wishing to cover the OFFICIAL WELCOME, or the ARRIVAL OF GUESTS, or the GRAND STAIRCASE, or the MIX N' MINGLE, please assemble at . . ." On the nights when I am the pool reporter—we have pools for covering state dinners, too—that's my cue to rush over to the mansion and try to snag some newsworthy quotes from the VIPs as they pass by on the other side of red velvet ropes. When I am not in the pool, I sit in the press room and wait for the exchange of toasts which is piped in over the loudspeaker, because only the pool reporters are permitted inside the State dining room to observe the toasts.

To the average NBC viewer I know that I appear to be a White House insider. There I am, standing on the mansion's front lawn looking self-assured, as though I've just come from a meeting with the President in the Oval Office, or perhaps from passing him in the hall on the way out the door. In fact, my meetings with the President, apart from meaningless photo opportunities, are almost as rare as a typical tourist's bumping into him on a Washington street.

Yet every day there are dozens of White House aides seeking to spread the presidential gospel on any number of issues. The very multiplicity of the issues gives the White House an advantage over journalists trying to present a more objective picture of government policies. For we are generalists. In the course of a week, or sometimes even a day, there may be important White House developments on national security, interest rates, energy, human rights, and a thorny labor issue. NBC, like other major news organizations, tries, as often as possible, to bring in our experts on stories that demand specialization. But there are just as many times when a staff reporter has to deal with a different set of complexities or nuances almost every day of the week. I suppose that can be frustrating, but it's also one of the really challenging and fun parts of my job. The old saying about variety being the spice of life may be a bit trite, but it has its applicability in the news business. One problem I never encounter is monotony.

Moreover, that gorgeous sprawling white mansion at 1600 Pennsylvania Avenue is an exciting place to spend one's days—even more so, I think, as an observer than as a participant. And every time I complain about long hours, elusive stories, demanding producers, duplicitous officials, or the rigidity of the clock, I try to remind myself of the rewards of working at the White House.

The Ninety-Second Movie

Television news is a hungry beast. Its strength is the emotional and visual impact of pictures—the unique capacity to make a news event come alive on the screen. Its weakness is that information typically must be tightly compressed into ninety-second news stories—an incredible requirement considering that approximately 50 million people regularly rely on the three network evening news shows to tell them what is going on in the world.

Producing a typical minute-and-a-half television news story on the "NBC Nightly News" is like producing a movie in brief, while always racing against the clock. Each spot must be reported, written, directed, and narrated by the correspondent; videotaped by one or more camera crews, often on different locations; packaged by the producer; edited by tape editors; and transmitted by microwave earth stations or telephone company video lines from points of origin throughout the world to network news headquarters in New York. Finally, all of the evening's spots must be shaped into a twenty-two-and-a-half-minute newscast by the program's producers. All this must be done within hours, sometimes minutes, with a subject matter that is inherently unpredictable and unruly. Thus the best efforts and intentions of daily television news coverage are always dominated by the final arbiter, the clock.

The networks go to extraordinary lengths to bring those

ninety-second news stories into viewers' living rooms. Capturing the video pictures, gathering the information, and fashioning it all into a typical news story consumes an inordinate amount of time, money, technology, and human energy. And whenever the story involves the President, the effort and expense increase staggeringly.

When President Jimmy Carter attended an economic summit in Tokyo in 1979, for example, NBC dispatched a team of four Washington-based correspondents, two Asia-based correspondents, economics reporter Irving R. Levine, five producers, three Washington-based crews, and tons of equipment to accompany him—along with rented time on an international telecommunications satellite to electronically "feed" the story back to New York.

When Carter took a break from the Oval Office to shoot the rapids of Idaho's Salmon River and go fishing in the Grand Tetons in Wyoming, in 1978, NBC went along to cover his trip, sending three correspondents, three producers, and two crews, and spending $50,000 to use a mobile satellite earth station, to transmit the story from the wilderness to "Nightly News" headquarters in New York.

And when Ronald Reagan retreats to his mountaintop ranch (which is off-limits to reporters) in California, NBC moves its White House news operation to Santa Barbara and perches camera crews in rotating shifts on a bluff overlooking the ranch to photograph the President's every move—from chopping and clearing brush to riding his favorite horse, "Little Man."

No other daily assignment in television news routinely commands convoys of correspondents, producers, cameramen, and technicians, or requires the technical capacity to broadcast within seconds from any corner of the globe.

It looked like a scene from the movie *M*A*S*H** that morning as the four huge military cargo helicopters hunkered down on the deck of the aircraft carrier, some fifty-five miles off the Southern California coast. But instead of airlifting medical evacuees, these helicopters were ferrying some news reporters, photographers, and broadcast technicians—a sort of Mobile White House Press Unit—to the U.S.S. *Constellation,* where President Ronald Reagan was paying a visit.

Newspapers, including such far-flung publications as the *Beverly Hills Courier* and the *London Daily Express,* each sent one reporter. The wire services, AP and UPI, and the news weeklies, *Time, Newsweek,* and *U.S. News and World Report,* each sent a reporter and a photographer. Nine radio networks sent correspondents and also sent technicians. Two local television stations each sent a correspondent and a two-person crew. But ABC, CBS, and NBC (which was providing the pool coverage that day) sent nine, seven, and ten representatives, respectively.

Judging from the marshalling of news-media manpower, you would have thought we were there to cover the President's address on a development of earth-shaking proportions. Actually, we were there to cover what amounted to a tightly scripted, three-hour-long, White House-produced photo opportunity, starring Ronald Reagan—who had once played commander Casey Abbott of the submarine *Starfish* in the movie *Hellcats of the Navy*—as Commander in Chief.

While television news cameras rolled, Reagan shook hands with officers and crew members; donned a baseball cap and commander's jacket that were presented to him; briefly took the *Constellation*'s helm; reviewed strafing runs, submarine hunts, and other shows of Navy air prowess put on for him; reaffirmed his pledge of "a Navy that is big enough to deter aggression wherever it might occur"; and pronounced his entire visit "a Yankee Doodle Day."

The President's visit was also a tailor-made-for-television day. Every detail, with the exception of the brilliant, blue Pacific sky, was carefully planned by the White House with an eye toward the network evening newscasts. Television obliged because, although it wasn't *Hellcats of the Navy,* it was a hell of a story, visually. And just to make sure that the story made the networks that night, the White House scheduled a helicopter shuttle especially for the three network television correspondents and their producers, who had to rush back in order to meet their evening news shows' deadlines.

Broadcasting may be the only business that is run on time, David Brinkley once noted. Under normal circumstances such punctuality is laudable, but when you consider that most news is inherently unpredictable and that there are four different time zones in the United States alone, you begin to understand the complications involved just in meeting a deadline.

Network news broadcasting is governed by Eastern Standard Time, no matter how many time zones separate the reporter from New York. Long before my producers, Jim Lee and Ray Cullin, and I landed at Santa Monica Airport at about two-thirty that afternoon, we had taken into account that the time was actually three hours later in the East. We started counting down the sixty minutes until the first broadcast of the "Nightly News" the instant we hit the ground. That day there was no time to spare for driving to the nearest studios, so the three networks had brought their studios to the airport. Three adjoining offices of an airplane hangar were transformed into three makeshift video-editing and sound-recording centers with three special telephone company video lines ready to feed the stories instantly to each network's broadcast center in New York.

Over the next hour, two NBC producers, three technicians, and I worked frantically, paring down more than an hour's worth of videotape into a one-minute-and-forty-five-second news "spot," or story.

If you've ever seen the elaborate gadgetry and slick efficiency of a television production studio, you would be aghast at the chaotic surroundings in which we managed to produce the White House story that day. For that matter, you would be aghast at the surroundings in which we produce *many* of our stories on the road. I've helped edit videotape in an open airport hangar during a dust storm. I've written scripts while holding a typewriter on my lap as I sat on the edge of a hotel bathtub—which happened to be the only available quiet corner. I've recorded soundtracks while sitting in a steamy car with the windows rolled up to block out the noise from the highway.

By comparison, producing this story from the airport was a piece of cake. While the technicians were cutting the spot in the editing room, I commandeered a desk and typewriter in the hall to write my script for the voice-over portion of the story. A large, half-open, steamer-type trunk, which was used to transport equipment, served as my "sound booth" while I recorded the tracks for the voice-overs as I stood in the hall.

We managed to finish feeding the story that day just fifteen seconds before the six-thirty edition of "Nightly News" went on the air. It was close, but we've cut it closer.

Producing a ninety-second news story on the White House isn't always this hectic, but rare is the day when the whole process doesn't come down to a race against the clock. Some days begin more slowly than others and lull you into thinking you have all the time you could possibly need. Then a story breaks late in the afternoon and suddenly you find yourself scrambling down to the wire to make your deadline. It's that kind of job.

Most days, I arrive at NBC's glass-enclosed cubicle in the White House press room between eighty-thirty and nine-thirty, unless I'm reporting for the "Today" show. On "Today" show mornings I must be there before six to tape my stand-up on the White House lawn as the sun rises.

Because of the overlapping demands of producing news reports for the morning shows, evening newscasts, and radio, and providing protective news coverage of the President, NBC, ABC, and CBS generally carve up the White House assignment along similar lines between two or more reporters. At NBC, radio reports and weekend television coverage are handled primarily by Andrea Mitchell. I rotate week-to-week with John Palmer between providing reports for the "Nightly News" and the "Today" show.

NBC's glass booth is one of a warren of identical cubicles which serve as "offices" for the White House correspondents assigned to them. The booth is barely large enough to accommodate one working reporter, but all three NBC correspondents manage to squeeze in, leaving room for only the essentials—the radio soundbooth, a work counter which holds three old Royal typewriters and three telephones, and a small portable TV set. My "files" are contained in the bulging briefcase I carry everywhere I go. My reference "library" is composed of dog-eared copies of *Congressional Quarterly, The Almanac of American Politics, Congressional Staff Directory*, and the facts I carry in my head.

Since the birth of my infant son, Jeffrey, I rarely have time to finish the morning papers at home before work. So usually the first thing I do at the office is read or at least scan the *Washington Post*, the *New York Times*, and the *Wall Street Journal*, looking mainly for new leads worth pursuing that day on continuing White House stories. After the papers, I glance at the President's agenda for the day to see if any meetings have been added since the preceding late afternoon, when the White House press office distributes his schedule to the news media. Then I check in with NBC's Washington bureau, the nerve center where all stories that originate in Washington are assigned, produced, and edited, along with the Washington portion of the "NBC Nightly News" with Roger Mudd. The bureau is located in the District of Columbia's northwest section, about a fifteen-minute drive from the White House and downtown Washington. But because I never leave the White House except to accompany the President or to go out for lunch or a quick errand, my contact with the bureau during the day is by telephone.

We first phone assignment editor George Cheely to make sure we have enough camera crews assigned to the White House that day to cover all the events on the President's schedule that are open to the media. Covering even the simplest event for television—a speech by the President in the Rose Garden, for example—usually requires one two-person camera-sound team to shoot the close-ups and record the sound, and another to shoot the wide shots and cutaways (background pictures that are interspersed with close-ups so as to provide a visual context for the tighter shots). So, we always have at least two crews at the White House. On an especially busy day, or when it's NBC's turn to provide pool coverage, we may add a third crew, or even a fourth.

Next I call the "Nightly News" producers in the Washington bureau, Russ Moore and John Holland, to discuss story ideas for that evening's show.

It's up to me to originate and select the stories I do, but it's the prerogative of the show's producers to decide whether to use them. Some days it's clear from the start that "Nightly" will want a piece from the White House, either because the President will be making news, or because an important announcement is expected from the Administration, or because of a development reported in the morning newspapers that demands a follow up. Other days, whether or not "Nightly" will want a White House piece depends on what news I am able to come up with by talking to sources.

A large part of any reporter's job is persuading editors and producers that a marginal story has enough merit to warrant space in the newspaper or time on the network newscast. But a television reporter must also convince producers that a story can be made visually interesting enough to hold viewer attention. A newspaper reader can skip over a boring story, but a television viewer is likely to switch to another channel.

Days when the story isn't readily apparent are often the most difficult because they involve long hours on the telephone with sources in an effort to dig up something newsworthy and numerous calls to producers in Washington and New York to keep them informed of my progress. Some days I scramble to come up with a story until four or five o'clock before "Nightly" 's producers decide they won't need anything from me. But from a reporting standpoint, these days are frequently the most interesting. I'm free to choose the story or stories I want to pursue without having to divide my time between attending "photo opportunities" and prearranged "news" events which may or may not produce anything of use but have to be covered. Preparing for the "Today" show is much the same.

Once the show producers agree that there is a story for "Nightly," I make the first of many calls to the producer in charge of overseeing the technical production of my spot to discuss the story's visual appearance. NBC has two producers permanently assigned to the White House—Jim Lee, who has been producing White House spots since I began covering the beat in January 1977, and Ray Cullin, who moved to the White House assignment in January 1981 from the NBC bureau in Burbank, California. Cullin and Lee are known as field producers, because a large part of their job is plotting the technical logistics of covering the President when he travels. On the road, they are asked to handle everything from arranging for the portable microwave earth station that transmitted the daily feeds to New York of President Carter's wilderness trip to setting up the temporary editing and transmission center at Santa Monica Airport. I am very fortunate to work each day with Lee or Cullin—in the television business, there are none better at what they do.

When the President is in Washington, the White House producers supervise technical production from the studio in the NBC bureau. As the day's news events unfold, we're in constant touch over the telephone. I keep my field producer advised of how I see the story shaping up; he advises me on the best videotape segments to illustrate my script.

Although I may witness a news event as it happens and while my crew records it, I sometimes don't see or hear the recorded tape until it is aired, because we have limited video playback facilities at the White House. As soon as the event is recorded at the White House, the videotape is shipped by courier to the bureau, or fed over video telephone lines, or by microwave, if it's late in the day. Once at NBC, it is screened by a White House producer, who acts as my eyes and ears when it comes to weaving the audio and video together into a news story. This sounds simple enough, but the process of tailoring the script to fit the pictures and vice versa can be a time-consuming and frustrating one, especially when the clock is ticking away toward my deadline. Some days it seems that I spend as much time coordinating pictures and script with my producer as I do actually reporting.

Let's say, for example, that I want to use a particular sound-bite from an interview with Senate Majority Leader Howard Baker, which was taped during a driveway stakeout as Baker left a meeting with the President that day. According to the notes I scrawled during the interview, that soundbite was Baker's most succinct or newsworthy statement and therefore the obvious choice for my story. But Lee, who screened the tape, may tell me that the soundbite of that quote is inaudible because the noise from a car pulling up the driveway drowns out what Baker said. Instead, Lee will suggest a more audible soundbite of Baker that fits with my script.

I also depend on my producer and NBC's assignment-desk people to keep me informed of what's going on elsewhere in Washington that may relate to that day's White House story. Maybe NBC's Capitol Hill correspondent managed to pry a few relevant words on camera from Ed Meese as he emerged from a Congressional hearing—but not enough to make a complete story. So, someone will alert me to the interview with Meese, and a producer will screen the tape and suggest possible soundbites for me to choose from.

Visually, White House television news spots tend to revolve around black limousines pulling up to and away from the west portico entrance because most days those comings and goings from the Oval Office are the only clues that reporters can glean of what went on behind closed doors. Just as the White House determines which events on the President's schedule are open to media coverage—usually merely photo opportunities—the White House also determines where we can set up our cameras and which areas are off-limits. The driveway is the only area within the White House gates where television reporters are free to conduct interviews with the cameras rolling. Such limitations, the White House says, are imposed because the President sometimes sees people whose visits he wishes to keep private. But reporters know that the Administration's desire to control the flow of news has as much to do with limiting television coverage as with concern for the President's privacy. Occasionally, those "private" visitors disagree with the President's views. Ushering them out a side door of the West Wing—far out of range of the cameras, whose daily vigil is limited to the front door—spares the President the political embarrassment of having a visitor emerge from the Oval Office as critical of the President's policies as when he entered. Sometimes the White House simply wants a meeting kept secret for diplomatic, security, political, or all these reasons.

The limitations imposed on television by the White House

increase the pressure on the reporter to make the story as visually interesting as possible, so that it comes alive on the screen. It's up to me to make sure that a crew is there at every White House stakeout, photo op, or scheduled event, so that I have the best pictures to work with. But very often White House stories are based on "not for quote" background statements by sources—for which there are no applicable pictures to illustrate the story—and the entire spot consists of my stand-up on the White House lawn. Even on the days when we are able to get officials speaking on the record and on camera, the resulting pictures are of people standing in the driveway or behind the podium of the briefing room. It's hardly the stuff of great television.

Covering the first year of the Reagan White House was particularly challenging from a visual standpoint, since much of the news was dominated by economic policy-making. Journalistically, the Reagan Administration's economic initiatives were as dramatic as the largely untested theories behind them were revolutionary. No Administration since the New Deal had matched the boldness and scope of Reaganomics and no Administration since the Great Society had matched the brilliance and muscle of Reagan's in ramming its economic package through Congress in those first months. But visually, the day-to-day reports on the progress of budget-cutting bills or tax-cut proposals provided little that was dramatic.

Making a television report on such a visually static story come alive on the screen sometimes calls for the use of video special effects. *Chyrons* (electronically enlarged words or numbers superimposed on the screen) might be used to illustrate and compare budget figures or to emphasize a quote. *Electronic still-storage,* which can make a still-frame picture from a videotape, might be used to create an image of a document on the screen, with excerpts superimposed in chyrons. A *blow back,* which reduces a picture on the screen to a box, might be used to break up a series of talking heads. A *page turn* can make a series of pictures on the screen appear to turn like pages in a book.

There's a fine line between dazzling viewers with special effects to the point where they distract from the story and using them to enhance a piece. It's up to the producer to know where to draw that line. But it's up to the correspondent to write the script to fit the special effects, so that the electronic graphics flow from the script rather than the script jumping from one illustration to the next. So, in addition to worrying about the quality of the visual material from the White House each day, I'm also constantly thinking about suggestions for graphic illustrations to accompany my story.

It's usually late morning, more than seven hours before the newscast, when the first videotape from the White House is delivered by courier to the Washington bureau. While I'm grabbing a sandwich at my desk, or working the telephones calling sources, or dashing from briefing to stakeout to photo opportunity, or pounding out the first draft of my script, the White House producer begins screening the first video cassettes.

In one typical day of covering the President, between six and eight twenty-minute cassettes are shot. Of that, maybe seventy seconds of video footage will be used in the average ninety-second spot. As the twenty-minute cassette is played back, the producer notes the exact time each picture appears on the tape, which he can do by watching the digital electronic timer attached to the editing machine. Screening the tape first saves precious time during editing later, when he may be working with several cassettes simultaneously. But it is sometimes not done because there isn't enough time.

When I'm covering an event on deadline with my crew, I keep an eye on my watch so that I know at what point a particular picture or soundbite appears on the cassette. Without ever actually viewing the tape, I can tell the producer exactly where to find that item.

The Ninety-Second Movie

Before the advent of the portable EJ (electronic journalism) camera in the early 1970s, television news cameras recorded events on film. Unlike video tape, which is broadcast-ready as soon as it is unloaded from the video tape recorder, film had to be processed and screened before it could be edited. A standard 400-foot reel, the typical load carried by television newsfilm cameras, would take at least forty-five minutes to an hour to process. Then the film had to be screened before it was edited, in order to determine where a particular picture or sequence appeared on the reel, because film is measured in feet or frames, not in terms of time. The reel was inserted into a viewer and the entire four hundred feet would have to be cranked through manually, frame by frame. The whole process was as time-consuming as it was laborious, and it normally required at least an hour to prepare a film-clip for broadcast.

Videotape, on the other hand, can be transmitted electronically in seconds and aired immediately. The networks rarely use unedited videotape on a newscast. But in fast-breaking news situations, such as the assassination attempt on President Reagan, videotape pictures of the event are frequently broadcast as soon as they are received, without even being edited first. On several occasions my closing stand-up has been inserted into a story and broadcast live as I delivered it from the White House lawn.

For me, the most challenging and frustrating aspect to making a story come alive on the screen is in the writing. To try to tell a complicated story in two hundred and fifty words or less—sometimes much less—requires a cool, decisive outlook. I'm not sure I'll ever grow entirely accustomed to leaving out information I think is important. But I have learned to grit my teeth when one of the show's producers tells me the script is too long and must be limited to ninety seconds or sometimes less.

A good television news script should be concise, comprehensible, and compelling enough to make viewers want to listen. But it also must be consistent in style and tone with the rest of the newscast. Writing for the "Nightly News" must normally conform to the plainspoken, straightforward style preferred by the show's producers and resident wordsmith, Gilbert Millstein. Essentially, "Nightly" prefers that the script stick to the facts as you know them, rather than try to be funny or clever. There is a distinction, though, between a correspondent's inserting his personality and adding his own insights or interpretations to a piece. Informed insight and balanced interpretation of the facts is essential to good reporting. Without those qualities, news reporting is reduced to a bland recitation of facts and press releases. But in television, those interpretations or conclusions are frequently reserved for the closing stand-up, the final summation which is supposed to neatly tie up the important points in the story like the bow on a package.

Writing for the "Today" show is a little more relaxed, a reflection of the time of day and the audience. "Today"'s viewers are people on the run. They're brushing their teeth, getting the kids off to school, gulping their coffee, with the television on in the background. They don't want to digest a lengthy or complicated news program. They want to know if anything important happened overnight that they should be aware of before getting on with their day.

Comparatively speaking, the other networks' news shows permit their correspondents more liberties with language. ABC's Sam Donaldson, for example, often uses funny lines and occasionally has even delivered his closings in rhyme and used homespun parables to make his points. But with a few exceptions—notably Tom Pettit's humorous and acerbic commentaries when he reported on Capitol Hill—not many correspondents at NBC can get away with trying to be clever in a straight news story.

Although I'm always thinking about the thrust and development of my story throughout the day, last-minute developments at the White House or late afternoon announcements and briefings usually preclude me from actually beginning to write the script much before four o'clock. Strangely, I find that the closer the deadline, the easier the script is to write. When time is short, I have to trust my instincts rather than mulling over what to leave in, what to take out, or whether there is a better way to say something. But there are days when I have to cut it closer than even I prefer—usually after I've been on vacation and I'm worried about being rusty.

My first day back after a three-month-long maternity leave of absence, the Reagan Administration announced, an hour before "Nightly" went on the air, that William Clark was replacing Richard Allen as the President's national security advisor. I had ten minutes in which to write the following script:

WOODRUFF NIGHTLY NEWS 1/4/82

Allen leaves house	Allen left his house in Virginia early this afternoon still denying that he planned to leave his job—despite suggestions for days from White House aides that that's exactly what they expected to happen.
Allen arrives W.H.	Allen avoided reporters when he arrived at the White House.
. . . leaves W.H.	. . . and when he emerged three and a half hours later.
Speakes/photo	It was very late in the day when White House spokesman Larry Speakes told reporters that Allen had submitted his

	resignation, by mutual agreement with the President.
W.H. report	Speakes said an internal White House investigation into Allen's conduct had cleared him completely—but that the public controversy surrounding Allen's receipt of cash and watches from Japanese journalists had led to the decision to remove him from his post. Speakes revealed Allen had accepted a temporary job, as a consultant to the President on foreign intelligence.
Briefing room/set up	The only person the White House made available for television cameras was Allen's replacement, as National Security Assistant, the current Deputy Secretary of State, William Clark. Clark told reporters that unlike Allen, who reported to White House counselor Edwin Meese, Clark will report directly to the President. He said he doesn't see continued feuding between the White House and the State Department.
SOT (sound on tape) *William Clark*	SOT (verbatim of Clark's comments)
WOODRUFF ON CAMERA	What no one said publicly was that Allen's fate was probably sealed months ago—even before the incident with the Japanese journalists, because he did not get along with senior aides James Baker and Michael Deaver. He had so little support from his White

House colleagues at the end, that they
joked he could probably find an outside
consultant's job, making a lot of money
from Japanese clients. Judy Woodruff,
NBC News, the White House.

After I've finished writing my script, I send it by telecopier
to the Washington bureau. Between the time I transmit the
text and the time I read it on the air, the script crosses the
desks of several different editor-producers. Russ Moore and
John Holland read it, as does Washington anchor Roger
Mudd. They are authorized to give final approval, but if the
producer in New York, Bill Wheatley, or executive producer
Paul Greenberg, feels strongly about a needed change, they
would weigh in as well.

Although the news anchors are the most visible people in
the show, the producers play a large role in shaping the newscast—from regulating the content and style of the stories to
determining the order in which they appear and the amount of
time allocated to each. An anchor reads the reports filed by
the correspondents in order to determine how to write the top
of the show and the lead-ins for the correspondents' reports.
But beyond that, his influence over story selection, order, and
the direction the stories take really depends on how much
control he chooses to exercise.

When John Chancellor anchored "Nightly News," he
would sometimes join in my phone discussions with a "Nightly"
producer and ask questions about my script and make helpful
suggestions or discuss a story. Chancellor was also involved in
selecting stories for the newscast. Roger Mudd, who is now
the co-anchor of "Nightly News," also deals with correspondents, even to the point of looking at their scripts. His influence has played a role in more focused and sharper reporting
by NBC's capital correspondents.

The script approval process is the critical juncture for a story. Some stories never make it past this point, usually because more pressing news edges them out. On a given day there may be as many as twenty correspondents vying for up to a dozen news spots that make up a twenty-two-and-a-half-minute "Nightly News" show, after you've subtracted time for commercials.

But it's an atypical day when "Nightly News" doesn't carry at least one White House story. Partly this is because the statements and actions of the President almost always make news, even if his Administration doesn't. A case in point was Ronald Reagan's month-long holiday at his ranch during the summer of 1981. Despite the President's determination that the vacation be a leisurely break from his official duties and as far removed from reporters as possible, all three networks went along to cover it, moving their White House news operations to nearby Santa Barbara.

Covering the President at the isolated "Ranch White House," which is actually a small adobe house at the end of a white-knuckle drive up a winding dirt road, posed special obstacles for all of the approximately twenty-five reporters who made the trip. For security reasons, and in order to assure the Reagans their privacy, reporters were not permitted on the mountaintop, much less the ranch, except when invited for the one photo opportunity scheduled during the President's stay there. But covering Reagan's vacation for television required elaborate preparations at an enormous cost.

The networks maintain what we call protective coverage of the President and what some ghoulishly refer to as a "death watch," even when the President is on vacation. This means that whenever the President ventures out, network television cameras always accompany him—either physically or electronically.

Since Reagan's outings at the ranch consisted mainly of

chopping and clearing brush and horseback riding over his 688 craggy acres, which were off-limits to reporters and television cameras, NBC set up a camera crew armed with a special, high-powered lens on top of a mountain that overlooks the ranch. The other networks, not to be outdone, quickly followed suit. When he heard about the cameras Reagan joked that he wondered what would happen if he suddenly clutched his heart during his next riding expedition. In addition to their mountaintop cameras, ABC, CBS, and NBC shared the cost of setting up an elaborate transmission-editing center and miniature newsroom, which occupied three rooms of a motel in Santa Barbara. Since Reagan frequently visits the ranch, the networks have permanently rented one room to store equipment in, in order to avoid having to pack it up and ship it each time the President stays at the ranch. More equipment is stored under platform beds in the other two motel rooms, which are rented to unwitting guests until the President's next visit.

After the script is approved by "Nightly" 's producers in New York, the technical side of "building" a White House spot begins. Some days it's nearly six o'clock before my producer and I are given the go-ahead—less than an hour until the show's first broadcast at 6:30 EST—and the entire production process becomes a race against the clock for the producer and tape editor. And on days when the story breaks late and involves combining videotape of several events, special effects, and possibly a live feed of my closing stand-up on the White House lawn, the cutting of a spot can resemble the countdown before a space shot.

Producing a ninety-second White House piece might involve four tape editors punching away at four editing-machine control panels: one editor cues up the soundbites selected by the producer during the preliminary screening; a second editor splices together the pictures and mixes the sound for the top half, while a third cuts the bottom half; and a fourth handles the live feed to the studio. Under that kind of pressure, a tape editor has to be decisive and he has to be fast. He must have the judgment to be able to look at five alternative shots and make the right choices without waffling. And he must have the skill to make the cuts without thinking about whether he's pushing the right button on the control panel. The mechanics of operating an editing machine must come to him as effortlessly as those of operating the brake pedal and clutch of a car, so that his attention is focused solely on the material. Some editors never get past the mechanics; others master the control panel but never develop an eye for the right picture. They don't last in network news very long.

Before the producer and tape editors begin editing the pictures, I record the soundtrack of my script in the radio booth at the White House. With the help of technician Aldo Argentieri at the White House, the soundtrack is instantly fed to the studio in the bureau, where it is "laid" in, or inserted electronically, as the voice-over narration that accompanies videotape pictures.

Often, just about the time the voice-over track is being laid, I'm racing out to the White House lawn, where a crew is waiting for me to perform my closing stand-up. I'm lucky if I've had a minute to run a brush through my hair and steal a glance in a mirror.

I take my position about four or five feet in front of the tripod camera which is pointed toward the front door of the White House. In the camera lens, I am a lone figure standing on the lawn with the mansion behind me forming a backdrop. What viewers at home don't see is that there are several other television correspondents, similarly positioned before their network's cameras, lined up on either side of me. Some days the lawn is so crowded with camera crews it resembles a studio back-lot, and it's difficult for me to hear myself delivering my script over the voices of the other correspondents. But because the White House confines us to this patch of lawn, we grin and bear it.

While the crew adjusts the lights and the camera-angle, I practice my closing lines so that I will be able to recite them without constantly shifting my eyes from the camera lens down to the paper in my hand, which can be distracting to viewers.

Performing before a television camera can be either as simple as remembering that it's something you enjoy or a hundred times more difficult. When I started at the White House I used to have butterflies before taping a stand-up. I was so concerned about delivering my lines flawlessly, with just the right inflections and pauses, that the NBC tape editors back in the bureau would mark time while they waited for me to finish by forming a betting pool on the number of takes I would have to do before I was satisfied. But now the butterflies occur only when I'm ad libbing during a live broadcast and there can be no retakes. I think even the most seasoned network reporters experience a touch of nervousness in those situations.

During a normal taping I look into the long black lens and think about the viewers who will be watching me—those same homemakers, executives, retirees, and students who send me letters—instead of just talking into an inert camera. I want them to stop what they are doing, to look at me and listen to what I am saying, because those closing lines are the summation of my story. But most of all, I want them to see me as being credible and authoritative, not just as someone who wandered out on the lawn to read a White House press handout.

Don't Touch That Dial

If there is one lesson that growing up as an Army brat taught me, it is how to cope. Whether it was the first day in a new school—and there were seven new schools between the first and seventh grades—or how to explain to my Taiwanese pedicab driver that I had lost the way, I learned early how to handle unfamiliar situations, or, at least, how to be something less than overwhelmed by them.

Coping with unfamiliar situations and issues is, in one sense, what being a reporter is all about. During the five years when I worked as a local television reporter in Atlanta and, later, as an NBC Atlanta bureau correspondent responsible for some 500,000 square miles of news, I reported stories that ranged from state-house politics to red-ant plagues. Once I even covered an execution on the Bahamian island of Nassau. Typically, I'd be sent on a story in mid-morning, and by the evening newscast I was expected to be an expert—or at least to appear to be one. At the White House, I report on the entire range of subjects competing for the President's attention, from supply-side economics to nuclear disarmament and social issues

Looking back, maybe my transient childhood helped prepare me for my baptism by fire in the news business as a young reporter. But the day this Army brat made the biggest move of her life—from emptying wastebaskets and fetching coffee in the newsroom of one Atlanta TV station to covering the Georgia state legislature for another—I was twenty-three years old and scared to death.

"I want you to go cover the statehouse today," the station's news director told me matter-of-factly. It was my second day on the job. (My first day, I had delivered an on-the-scene report on a highway dispute from the median strip.) All I knew about reporting was what I had picked up looking over reporters' shoulders in the newsroom while working in my previous job as a gofer and newsroom secretary at a competing station, although I *had* been on one other assignment: I held a microphone while another reporter conducted an interview.

To make matters worse, I knew little more about Georgia state politics than I did about reporting. Did I tell my boss? Are you kidding?

I had been angling for the chance to be a television reporter for more than a year, and I wasn't going to permit cold feet and inexperience to stand in my way now. I put on my most confident face and set out for the opening session of the state legislature. Fortunately, the cameraman who was sent out with me, Leroy Powell, was both a television and statehouse veteran. He introduced me to the people I needed to know and told me how to hold the microphone and where to position myself during the stand-up. With the help of this crash course in television journalism, I somehow muddled through my first political reporting assignment. Up-close, in-depth, and in ninety seconds, I interviewed two state legislators on the big issues facing the assembly during the upcoming session. I watched myself on the newsroom monitor that night, feeling embarrassed and inadequate.

Boy, did I have a lot to learn.

I am not one of those people who started out early in life knowing exactly what I wanted to be. Instead, I wanted to be everything: all-American girl, straight-A student, class president, and college thespian, career woman and wife and mother. Growing up as an only child until I was eight and being the center of my parents' attention provided me with a healthy dose of self-confidence. There was never any doubt that I would go to college, even though no one else in my family had. I grew up believing that people can accomplish whatever they want, if they set their minds to it.

As I look back, I realize that the sense of self-confidence and ambition my parents cultivated in me probably gave me strength when setbacks seemed to overshadow successes early in my career. There is a widespread belief in television news that the trick to getting ahead is being in the right place at the right time. And while it's true that many a reporting career has been boosted by providence, it's equally true that success in television news has a lot to do with tenacity. It's a business that can be as shattering as it can be rewarding, I've found, and you have to be able to learn from your setbacks.

My parents also taught me that life's rewards came to those who worked hardest and were willing to take a few risks along the way. My father, William Henry Woodruff ("Woody" to his friends), left Roanoke Rapids, North Carolina, while still a teenager, inspired by a recruiting poster on the wall of the town post office and the time-worn adage: Nothing ventured, nothing gained. Joining the Army was his escape from an almost certain career in the local cotton mill. He rose through the infantry ranks during World War II and retired as a warrant officer. My mother, Anna Lee Payne, dropped out of school when her father died and began working as an elevator operator to help support her three younger siblings. My parents met and married while Dad was stationed at Fort Sill, Oklahoma. I was born one year later.

For my parents, the travel and new friends afforded by military life were exciting opportunities that more than made up for the disruptions and homesickness. My father's rank and the strength of American prestige (as well as the American dollar) assured that we lived well abroad. While overseas we sacrificed none of the customary amenities of American life and even acquired a few new-found luxuries, including live-in help.

I knew little outside military life until I was thirteen years old. It never occurred to me that celebrating my fifth birthday aboard ship while crossing the Atlantic was the ultimate birthday party. Nor did I consider attending kindergarten in the country that invented the word and learning to speak German to be rare cultural opportunities. Speaking German was the only way to communicate with most of my playmates in Mannheim. And when we were transferred to Kaohsiung, Taiwan, in 1956, I didn't consider the tiny, underdeveloped country to be a hardship post. As a ten-year-old, I found Taiwan's primitive way of life fascinating. Outside the high wall which surrounded our modern, Western-style house my two-year-old sister, Anita, and I used to wait for the peasants who worked in the surrounding rice paddies to begin their march home at day's end so we could see their plow oxen. When the monsoons flooded the rice paddies and transformed our walled garden into a moat, we imagined that our house was an island and that we were shipwrecked sailors. My mother, meanwhile, fretted about typhoid.

But it's curious, considering my eventual career choice, that those years overseas meant that much of my childhood was spent isolated from television at a time when my contemporaries were emerging as the first kid-vid generation. During the two years we lived on Taiwan, my family owned one of the few television sets on the island. And only once do I remember its actually working. That day, with the help of a makeshift antenna my father rigged using scrap wire, we were able to pick up a snowy broadcast of a Doris Day movie from

Manila. Our maintenance man, Jack, took one look at the moving images on the screen and ran from the room as though he had seen a ghost. I'm not sure what affect, if any, television had on me while I was growing up, except that I came to regard it as something of a novelty. But I do know the affect it had on Jack. Despite my father's attempts to explain, in halting Chinese, the electronic principles that made this magic, Jack thereafter was always wary of the room where the TV was located.

In a way, my return to the States in 1957, when my father was transferred to Fort Gordon, near Augusta, Georgia, turned out to be a greater culture shock for me than Taiwan ever had been. Although I was accustomed to moving to new places and making new friends, sometimes in the middle of a school year, I had never felt disadvantaged by it before moving to Georgia. Previously, my peer group consisted mostly of other military kids who were all as eager to make friends as I was. Now, as a twelve-year-old in Augusta, I was thrown in with civilian kids who had grown up in this small Southern town and had gone to school together since kindergarten. Outsiders were kept at arm's length. I felt torn between wanting the acceptance of my peers and feeling that I was perhaps a little superior, if only because I didn't *need* that acceptance. There was never any doubt in my mind that I was just passing through Augusta.

I set about trying to resolve the conflict by overachieving with a vengeance during my junior and senior high school years, figuring that my accomplishments would ensure acceptance by my peers—but on my terms. The results were mixed. I tried out for, and didn't make, the varsity cheerleading squad. But I was accepted into the high school sorority, drama club, and community theater. I won the Augusta Junior Miss Pageant, but lost my bid for vice-president of the student council. And so I attained a measure of acceptance. But on reflection, I realize that I also unwittingly gained something far more important from the little extracurricular victories of those tender years: a curious blend of insecurity and resiliency, a feeling that I could survive—and in fact succeed—on my own. I didn't need somebody to take care of me, to show me the way. I could make it by myself.

As my family settled into Augusta's quiet, relaxed way of life after my father's retirement, I dreamed of colleges far away, and tried to focus on a career that would both serve my fellow man and help keep me fulfilled. Just where I was headed I didn't know, but I reasoned that I needed a degree from a top university to get there. I set my sights on Duke University. While I waited for word of my acceptance, I was awarded a scholarship at North Carolina's Meredith College, a small Baptist women's school with a good academic reputation. The scholarship persuaded me to start out at the smaller school and find my academic bearings there first. After two years of majoring in mathematics at Meredith, I transferred to Duke, where I earned a degree in political science.

I entered the news business through the back door when I was hired as a $90-a-week news secretary for Atlanta's WQXI-TV, an ABC affiliate. I was casting about for a career in the fall of 1967 before my graduation from Duke the next June, and television news fascinated me—a logical choice for someone with a political science degree who didn't want to teach or attend graduate school.

I had learned what little I knew about reporting from a few courses on politics and mass communications, and from observing reporters during two summers I spent in Washington. In 1966 and 1967, before my junior and senior years, I was selected as a Congressional student intern in the office of my home district congressman, conservative Democrat Robert Stephens, after I wrote to him expressing my interest. Those months in Washington were revelatory—my first glimpse of a world filled with exciting, interesting people whose ambitions seemed to have more to do with making their mark than with merely making a living.

Journalism, it seemed to me then, was a field that attracted some of the best and the brightest in Washington. More important, journalism seemed to offer an opportunity to touch the lives of others, and, being an idealist, I wanted to "do good." It also seemed to me at the time that television held better opportunities for an aspiring young reporter than did newspapers, particularly for one who hadn't been trained as a writer. Even the most casual viewer during the sixties could see that TV was a news medium that was growing in size as well as influence. It was television to which the country turned for the stories of political assassinations, civil rights marches, urban riots, student demonstrations, and the battlefield of the Vietnam War. Television news was at the center of these explosive, turbulent times.

Breaking into television, I figured, wasn't much different from getting started in most fields. I could try to start at the top, in this case New York or Washington, and risk getting lost in a more experienced crowd. Or I could start at the bottom—possibly even on the air—in some remote place, and risk getting lost in obscurity. I decided to compromise and shoot for the middle. I wanted a city that was large enough to provide varied and interesting news but small enough to provide the opportunity to learn a new business. I narrowed the choice to Atlanta, a large city in the South, a part of the country I felt I had come to know during the nine years I had lived there.

In the spring before my college graduation I wrote to the three network-affiliated stations in Atlanta, promising that what I lacked in experience I would more than make up for with enthusiasm and willingness to work. All three stations' news directors wrote back, thanking me for my interest, but only one, Bill Conover of WQXI-TV, was willing to grant me an interview. With the money I had earned working as a part-time file clerk in the Duke admissions office, I flew to Atlanta during spring break. I had already mailed Conover what I hoped would be my passport to a job in television news: a perfectly typed resume chock-full of my proudest accomplishments: dean's list, Congressional internship, Alpha Delta Pi sorority member.

My first clue that WQXI was the stepchild of Atlanta television came as the car I was in turned off Peachtree Street. Before me stood a stately, white-columned, Georgian-style building surrounded by a rolling, manicured lawn. That, the driver told me, was station WSB-TV, the NBC affiliate which, I would later learn, dominated Atlanta television news. Next door, housed in a drab, cement-block building surrounded by an asphalt parking lot which overlooked the freeway, was WQXI-TV.

I waited in the lobby until Conover, a wiry man with thinning gray hair and a flushed face, came out to meet me. We sat and talked, and after about ten minutes he told me I was hired. "Besides," he added, grinning, "How could I turn down somebody with legs like yours?"

As it turned out, good legs were the best qualification for the job, since I spent most of my day running for coffee and for the telephone. I took calls from press agents announcing "news" conferences as well as viewers complaining about stories or the interruption of sports events. I cleaned film and kept up the film file. In between, I was always looking over reporters' shoulders and asking questions. More than once, I was told to "stay out of the way" as I hovered over the anchorman's desk, asking him why he decided to lead with a particular story.

While this wasn't exactly the journalistic job that I had had in mind, I told myself that at least I had my foot in the door. Because WQXI was permanently locked in the cellar of Atlanta news ratings at the time, it seemed a good place to start. Anywhere I went from there had to be up. With the smallest news staff of the three network affiliates, WQXI devoted the least amount of air time to local news and, I suspect, the least amount of money to news-staff salaries. My $90 a week barely covered my half of the rent for a one-bedroom apartment I shared with a college girlfriend. To make ends meet, I took a second job working a few nights a week as a typesetter in a printing firm.

I was also encouraged by the fact that news secretary could be considered the first step toward becoming a television reporter at the station—if you were a woman, that is. Coming out of college, I expected I'd have to start lower and work harder because I was a woman, no matter what career I chose. That was simply a given. And I was aware that, in those days, Nancy Dickerson was among the very few women reporters covering politics at the network level, which was my ultimate goal.

But I assumed that, once I'd proved myself by working hard and learning my craft, my sex would be irrelevant. What I hadn't understood was just how difficult it would be to move beyond discrimination. In 1968 women in local television news were regarded more as window dressing than as reporters. The consensus was that you needed a woman on camera, but there weren't enough Junior League bake sales or PTA meetings to cover to justify hiring more than one. The idea that a woman could cover serious news or politics was practically unheard of. According to the conventional wisdom, women were nice to look at, but they lacked authority on the air. And for many years that attitude was the self-fulfilling legacy of women in television. How could women possibly have credibility on the air, when men were hiring them primarily on their looks?

During my first few months at WQXI I badgered news director Conover to make me a reporter. And from the beginning, he replied that the station already had a woman reporter. She was blonde, buxom, bubbly, and, of course, assigned to women's features. There was no way around the fact that my future at the station was inextricably bound up with hers, and she seemed very content to stay where she was. I began answering the job ads in *Broadcasting* magazine. Invariably, the maddening replies I received from news directors around the country were always the same: "We're not looking for a woman. We're looking for a reporter."

I had been at the station about a year and was thinking about leaving Atlanta to try my luck starting at the bottom some place else, when the weekend weather announcer was fired. The new news director suggested I try out for her regular Sunday night slot on the eleven o'clock newscast. No thanks, I told him; I wanted to be a political reporter, not a weather girl. He took me aside and bluntly explained that if I ever wanted to get any on-the-air experience at WQXI, I'd better go for it. Besides, he said, there was the matter of the raise I had been angling for. Well, here was my chance to earn a whopping $150 a week, enough so that I could quit moonlighting as a typesetter.

I auditioned for the job, my first appearance on camera, by reading a batch of weather wire copy. Probably more because I was available, cheap talent than because of my performance, I was hired to fill four to five minutes each Sunday night discussing the finer points of high- and low-pressure systems. I hated every minute. I knew I wasn't fooling anyone with my flimsy knowledge of meteorology. I was there to add color to the scenery and tell viewers whether they should wear their galoshes tomorrow.

When I heard a few months later that the women's features reporter at rival WAGA-TV was leaving to have a baby, I didn't waste any time in phoning WAGA's news director, Bob Brennan. Without mincing words, I told him I wanted the job. To my relief, he invited me to come in for an interview and an audition.

At the time, WAGA, a CBS affiliate, was growing rapidly under the direction of Brennan, a former CBS field producer who had been hired to build the station's news operation and to give leader WSB a run for its money. Atlanta station owners, like their counterparts throughout the country, were beginning to discover that there was huge money to be made in local news. Until now the primary reason for producing a local news show was to satisfy the Federal Communications Commission, which issued and could revoke broadcast licenses. Any station that expected to keep its license had to fulfill the FCC requirement of carrying a certain amount of programming "in the public interest, convenience, and necessity." Much early local news programming was produced with the minimum effort and cost required to satisfy the FCC's requirement. As recently as the late 1950s, TV newscasts consisted mainly of talking heads reading the news in the studio: an anchor, a sportscaster, and a weathercaster. Still, even with these barebones news operations, most local news programs lost money. And so there was no incentive for stations to expand news staffs or coverage.

By the late 1960s and early 1970s, however, local television news had become an asset rather than a liability for many stations. What pushed the local evening newscast into the asset column of the ledger was the crucial role it played in building up evening audiences early, which surveys had shown was the key to assembling blocs of viewers for prime time, when advertising rates were highest.

At the forefront of this turnaround stood the market researchers and the "show doctors." The marketing people told station managers the size of their audiences (their "audience

ratings") and who their viewers were in terms of such demo-
graphics as age, sex, race, education, and income level. This
was valuable information with which to approach advertisers,
if your station was lucky enough to have the highest ratings
among the most coveted purchasing bloc, the eighteen to forty-
nine age group. And if your station wasn't number one, you
went out and hired a television news consultant, or show
doctor, to tell you how to package your newscast to attract a
greater share of that prized group.

At the same time that WAGA hired Bob Brennan, the
station brought in one of the top television news consultants,
McHugh & Hoffman Inc., to shape the appearance and, to a
degree, the content of the station's newscasts. Part of the
packaging called for hiring women. Marketing surveys had
shown that women made the decisions in the family when it
came to selecting television channels or shows, and that more
women than men tuned into the early evening newscasts. So
the idea was to select on-the-air talent that women viewers
would find appealing or with whom they could identify.

The day I walked into Bob Brennan's office I had little
knowledge of television ratings or show doctors, and I knew
nothing of the behind-the-scenes changes at WAGA that would
eventually lead to my promotions and demotions there. Once
again, I brought a resume. But this news director read it. He
seemed impressed by the fact that I had graduated from Duke,
studied political science and a year of Russian, and interned
in Congress. And when I told him flatly that I wanted to cover
hard news, he didn't try to talk me out of it.

For my audition, he handed me a stack of wire copy and
told me to rewrite it into a script, then to read the script as
though I were delivering a newscast. This, he explained, was
to see if I could write and perform as a reporter. Next, he
told me to talk about myself on camera, as though there were
an audience out there I was trying to reach. He said that this

was to see if I "came through the glass." I had never written a script before. But I remembered that a TV reporter at WQXI once told me that you should write for television the way you speak. Relying on that advice and what I knew about syntax and grammar, I improvised a script and tried to read it the way I imagined Walter Cronkite would. I ad libbed the second half as I went along, trying to conceal my nervousness.

When I left Brennan's office that day, I made up my mind that if I didn't get the job I was going to pack my bags and look for work in another city. It was a decision made out of desperate resignation, not arrogance. I didn't expect to get the job. A few days later, when Brennan called to tell me I was hired, I was too flabbergasted to ask him when I was supposed to start.

Bob Brennan's approach to training young reporters was the sink-or-swim school. He sent them out their first day on the job with veteran cameramen, figuring that if they didn't grasp the basics then, they never would. When you were fielding a young news staff that was roughly half the size of your leading competitor's, there wasn't time to lead anyone by the hand while you explained the finer points of broadcast journalism. And so my first lesson in TV reporting was that there would be no crash course in Journalism 101 as I had expected when I walked into WAGA's newsroom that January day in 1970. Instead, I found myself promptly dispatched to the scene of a property dispute involving a rural area called Henry County. From then on, everything I learned about reporting I learned by trial, error, and osmosis.

Fortunately, Brennan was a patient and understanding boss and WAGA was a place where you could make mistakes. But at the time I felt less reassured than pressured. I was keenly aware that I was regarded by some as a token, hired more because of my sex than my ability. And I felt that my mistakes would be seized on by some as proof that I was an empty-headed blonde, further evidence that women just couldn't cut it in serious news.

During those first few months every day was a struggle. My feeling that I was never adequately prepared and that I was always running to catch up with more experienced reporters was compounded by the frenetic, grab-and-run coverage of my statehouse beat. If there was an important bill being debated in the House and a vote being taken in the Senate, I had to choose which one to cover because we rarely had a second available crew. On days when the legislature ran late, we had to concede important stories in order to make our deadlines. The film we used in those days had to be into the station and ready for processing at least forty-five minutes before we were ready to edit. Typically, my cameraman, Leroy, and I would be leaving the state capitol in downtown Atlanta just in time to hit the crosstown rush hour. There were many hair-raising rides back to the station with Leroy driving while I wrote my script in my lap and prayed that we would make it safely and in time to get our film processed.

I learned news judgment under the same deadline pressures. Most of the time, it was up to me to decide what Atlanta-area viewers needed to know about the issues or decisions confronting their state legislature that day. When I reduced a complicated issue or day-long floor debate to a two-minute news story, no editor questioned my accuracy or conclusions. By the end of the day, editing film took precedence over editing copy. As the reporter, I was simply trusted to represent what was accurate and fair. It was a heavy responsibility at the time, even more so as I look back on it, and a very risky practice for any news organization. Chasing deadlines from day to day doesn't leave much time for reporters to reflect on how balanced their coverage is or on the legal ramifications of their methods of obtaining a story. As a result, some things made it on the air in those days in local television which never should have and probably would not today. But there were also many stories that I was proud of.

During the summer of 1974 I reported a controversial series of stories on housing discrimination. One included an on-camera confrontation between me and an apartment manager that resulted in her threatening to sue the station for broadcasting the incident without her permission. Acting on a tip that the federally subsidized apartment complex discriminated against blacks in its rental practices, I enlisted a black news secretary to pose as an apartment hunter and we drove to the building with a crew. Our secretary inquired about an apartment and was told by the manager that there were no vacancies. But when my white cameraman inquired, he was promptly shown an available apartment.

A few minutes later, I knocked on the startled apartment manager's door with my crew and—with the camera still rolling—confronted her with the discrepancy in her answers. After the story aired, I received several threatening phone calls from white viewers, some of whom shouted obscenities.

In the summer of 1971, some eighteen months after I had started at the station, I felt I had learned many of the nuts and bolts of television news. If I wasn't a veteran reporter, I was at least a journeyman. But that summer I was named to my first news-anchor job, a promotion which opened a whole new side of the business. This was when I first became aware of ratings. Until then, I was too preoccupied with proving myself to give much thought to the audience, apart from trying to convey a sense of authority and credibility on the air. But now, I came to find, that wasn't enough. I had to be concerned about whether viewers *liked* me—a vague estimation that the station management seemed to feel had to do with my ability to personify some collective viewer fantasy.

And that, they determined, had to do with the length of my hair, the style of my clothes, and my ability to be chatty on camera.

Six months after I began anchoring the thirty-minute noon newscast, we pulled ahead in the ratings from number two behind perennially preeminent WSB. It was the first time that anyone could remember another station knocking WSB out of first place. Much of the credit for that success has to do with the fact that we were simply producing a better show, thanks to Phyllis Mueller, who began producing the newscast when I began anchoring it. The noon news had long been regarded by Atlanta stations as the "women's newscast," which meant that it was heavy on fluff: horoscopes, diet crazes, and the latest goings-on in the lives of movie stars. But we emphasized consumer news, product safety, and self-help stories. Because the noon show was a low priority for the station was concerned, we were given free rein in shaping it.

Largely because of the noon news ratings, I became the first woman to co-anchor WAGA's evening newscast, presumably to see if I could work the same alchemy with its ratings. It was a giant leap in status, but a sharp decline in control over the newscast I was presenting.

The local evening newscast was the station's broadcasting signature. WAGA's identity, prestige, and an increasing share of its profits were pinned on the sixty minutes that preceded the "CBS Evening News." And that meant that an increasing amount of the station management's attention and the show doctor's tinkerings were focused on the show and the "news team," as they juggled and packaged in a vain effort to find the magic formula that would make WAGA number one. They wanted more "action" stories—fires, murders, accidents—and a faster pace for the show. Stories became shorter (the better to appeal to a presumably limited viewer-attention span), and "lighter" (viewers were bored by serious or complicated stories). We were shown tapes from New York of WABC's pioneering "Eyewitness News," with its blazer-jacketed, happy-talk news team—anchor Roger Grimsby, sportscaster Howard Cosell, and weatherman Tex Antoine, and its emphasis on "action-oriented" film stories. I remember an "Eyewitness News" film report on a multiple murder in which the camera traced the path of blood from victim to victim. At the time, we were told "Eyewitness News" was killing the other two network flagship stations in the New York market ratings. And this, we were told, was the kind of newscast, the kind of coverage, we were to emulate.

But first we had to look and act the part. We were given gray blazers with Channel 5's insignia on the breast pocket. We were told to ad lib more and act like we enjoyed each other's company on the air. Weatherman Guy Sharpe continued reading his mail on camera and bringing in pies that various ladies' auxiliaries had baked for him. I was sent to the station manager's wife's favorite stylist for a haircut. I didn't see what my hair had to do with the ratings, but it clearly had to do with my keeping the co-anchor position, so I reluctantly submitted to an ear-length shearing by Mr. Donald.

During the slightly more than a year that I co-anchored the evening news, we were still number two and Bob Brennan was replaced as news director by Pat Polillo, a man in a hurry to make his reputation. The obvious place to start was the evening newscast. Polillo looked at the ratings, looked at the show, looked at the news team, and decided I had to go. I was crushed. I thought they were trying to tell me that my career was finished at age twenty-six, that I couldn't cut it. For days I brooded, wondering what I had done wrong. But the more I thought about it, the more I realized that I hadn't done anything wrong. Maybe I wasn't the greatest anchor. Maybe I wasn't the fastest with the happy-talk quips. But what had they done to help me become better?

I was still the noon news anchor and the statehouse reporter, and I decided to work even harder and to improve my reporting skills. I became involved in stories on block-busting which grew into an award-winning series. I appeared regularly on a local Public Broadcasting System show, "Atlanta Week in Review," as a statehouse expert. And I fired off letters of inquiry to network-owned-and-operated stations, which seemed less intimidating than trying to get a job directly with a network.

But now more than ever, a network correspondent's position in Washington loomed as a distant goal. During the six years since I had started out as a news secretary, there had been an explosion of opportunities for women in television, sparked by pressures from the FCC on both local stations and the networks to hire more women and minorities, and aided by a spate of lawsuits by women's groups charging discrimination. I had a sense that the networks might be looking for more women reporters. With my experience as an anchor and political reporter, I figured I was as good a candidate as any.

When Atlanta's PBS affiliate sent me to Washington in November 1974, I decided to go up to New York and talk to all three networks about job possibilities. The most encouraging response I received was from NBC, where I was interviewed by Dick Fischer, then a network vice president. "You need to work on your voice," he told me. "It's too soft and too Southern. Call us in six months." My voice? Nobody had ever said anything to me about my delivery, and I had never thought of myself as speaking with an accent. I felt a bit like I'd been thrown a curve ball or, worse, like I was being given the brush off.

When I returned to Atlanta, I discussed how to improve my delivery with a colleague, who explained the network's preference for broadcasters who spoke with no trace of a regional dialect. He suggested a local voice coach, whom I called right away and arranged to meet in a day or two.

A week or so later, Fischer called, telling me there was an unexpected opening for a reporter in NBC's Atlanta bureau.

He offered me the job. I accepted without hesitation, and never made more than two sessions with the voice coach.

I was hired as one of two correspondents in NBC's Atlanta bureau who were assigned to cover ten states and the Caribbean. Our beat was an approximately 500,000 square-mile area which ranged from Louisiana to North Carolina, from Kentucky to Jamaica. I found that I spent more time in transit than I did at home. And I found that I had a lot to learn about television reporting. It was one thing to cover stories for a local station, but quite another to do stories the way a network wanted them done.

Each network has its own standards for story length and style. The enforcer of NBC's writing standards was Gilbert Millstein, a *New York Times*-trained editor for the "Nightly News." Millstein had very definite ideas about what kind of script was acceptable; and he was a stickler for grammar. My script rarely coincided with his ideas. I had to learn how to write into a story (that is, to leave room for the anchor to do a lead-in), and how to write to the pictures (meaning that a reporter shouldn't talk about the town mayor's meeting while the screen shows a picture of the mayor walking down the street).

A typical argument with Millstein involved a story I did on a Bicentennial celebration in a small south Georgia town. In my close, I wrote, "The people gathered round the music show."

"You can't *gather round* something," Millstein told me. "You either gather or you form a circle around." I argued that it was a commonly used expression and that I was trying to evoke mood. The producer came on the phone and overruled Gil.

"You won," Gil said, "but I'll kill you if you ever write 'gather round' again."

I should mention that we rarely have such arguments today

because I have since learned to write to suit Gil's style. We've also become good friends.

Then there was learning the technical side of television news: going to a strange affiliate and arranging to have my story fed to the network; learning what it meant when the "loop" (the telephone line used for video transmission) was down and you didn't get a piece fed by six o'clock.

It seemed that I was always at the mercy of the telephone lines, the airline schedules, and the vagaries of editors' whims. I remember covering a school-board controversy in a little town in South Carolina as a typical day: I left at seven A.M, the first available flight, and arrived at noon. . . . Hurried over to do the interviews—a civil rights spokesman, a black parent, a white parent, school-board officials. . . . Made sure the crew had pictures of the school and the neighborhood. . . . Drove thirty miles or so to the nearest NBC-affiliated station to edit and feed the video to New York—thirty minutes to deadline and I'd just begun to edit the piece and write my script. . . . Sent the script up to New York. . . . Gil Millstein and I went round and round on the telephone, as the pictures were fed. Finally, we struck a compromise. . . . "Nightly" decided not to use the piece. I was crushed for the rest of the day, but tried not to think about it as I raced for the airport to catch the last flight back to Atlanta in order to sleep in my own bed. The next day, I started all over again.

Instead of the exciting, career-advancing step I had envisioned, I found that working as a network bureau correspondent was draining, even at times demoralizing. There was no time for anything but work. On a moment's notice, I would have to cancel dinner plans to fly somewhere to cover a story. I lived out of a suitcase. Just getting my laundry done and shopping for groceries became the primary concerns of what was left of my private life. I began to have serious doubts about how much longer I could continue at that relentless pace, about whether I was cut out for the news business at all. I thought about quitting, but to do what?

Those were the thoughts spinning in my head that spring of 1975 after Jimmy Carter had declared his intention to seek the Democratic nomination for president. The resounding reaction from the national news media was to ask, "Jimmy who?" and then to disregard the incident as one man's folly. But I knew Jimmy Carter from covering him during his one-term governorship of Georgia, while I was reporting on the statehouse for WAGA-TV. I took him very seriously. I had kept an eye on the Carter forces, watching political strategist Hamilton Jordan go to work in Washington at Democratic National Committee headquarters under chairman Bob Strauss. He had spent a year building grass-roots support for Carter, thanks to his contacts with fifty Democratic state party chairmen. I knew that Carter himself had been building political contacts, too, by traveling around the country making speeches on behalf of other Democratic candidates. I had watched him charm church and civic groups as he stumped in and around Atlanta. "I'm Jimmy Carter and I think it's time for a fresh face in government," he would tell them, as he shook their hands. And by the end of the evening he would have his audience believing he cared about each and every one of them.

Whenever I suggested to my editors in New York that we ought to pay more attention to Carter, they laughed. Then, in the fall of 1975, "Nightly News" ordered a series of profiles of the presidential candidates. Because Terry Sanford, the former governor of North Carolina, and Carter were in my region, I was assigned to profile them.

As Carter started to sweep the primaries with me in tow as the NBC correspondent assigned to cover him, "Jimmy Who" began to emerge as the media darling of 1976. Well-known political writers from New York and Washington and the major news organizations from around the country suddenly converged on the Carter campaign, hailing the previously ignored peanut farmer from Plains as the presidential front-runner. My fortunes seemed to be soaring with Jimmy Carter's. The thrill of covering the leading candidate in my first national political campaign naturally assuaged my earlier doubts about my job, although I was working and traveling harder than ever. But now my distant goal of covering politics in Washington seemed within reach.

Then, in March 1976, the NBC assignment editor in New York called to tell me I was off the Carter campaign. "We want to give everybody a chance to cover the front-runner," he said, adding that veteran reporter Don Oliver was replacing me. I knew that what he really meant was that he didn't think I was experienced enough to cover Carter now that he was on top. Ever since Carter had won the Iowa caucus, I had been hearing that other, more senior NBC reporters were angling for my assignment, suggesting that they didn't think a rookie should have it. But I had naively failed to heed those warnings.

"I think you're making a mistake," I told him. "I have good contacts among the Carter people." But I knew even as I spoke that my fate was sealed for now; all I could do was wait and hope for another chance to prove myself.

For the next eight weeks I was assigned to cover, on an irregular basis, the flagging campaigns of George Wallace and Senator Henry "Scoop" Jackson. There was little doubt in anyone's mind at that point that the presidential aspirations of both were going nowhere.

By late May, with the Democratic convention and a certain nomination for Carter just a month off, covering his campaign had grown into a two-reporter job. And so I again found myself assigned to the Carter campaign, only this time as Don Oliver's back-up. This meant that I normally got on the air only for "Today" show pieces. Still, I was rapidly becoming the company expert on Carter and the people around him. Whenever somebody was doing a special or an interview on Carter, they would call me for information or depend on me to introduce them. It seemed that my Carter contacts were paying off for everybody but me.

I spent the summer of 1976 in Plains, Georgia, following the less-than-momentous comings and goings of the Democratic presidential nominee-to-be. Carter returned to his tiny hometown after emerging from the primary season all but assured of victory at the upcoming convention in New York.

Summers in Plains can be hardship duty, unless the visitor enjoys stifling heat and humidity. Stakeouts at the Carter home meant covering little Amy's lemonade stand and keeping an eye peeled for the future president's occasional strolls down Main Street. Besides covering his trips to Sunday School and church on the weekend, this particular summer also meant witnessing busloads of economic or foreign policy experts, made humble by the dusty, three-hour ride from Atlanta, step down on the dirt road in front of Miss Lillian's pond house, where they had been invited to brief Carter as he formulated policy.

Stories about members of the Carter family abounded that summer: Miss Lillian and her irreverent wit; cousin Hugh and his worm farm; sister Gloria and her motorcycle; brother Billy and his beer. Many of the relationships that would haunt the President in the White House were obvious here.

There were few stories of substance for the press corps to pursue. One involved Billy's purchase of hundreds of acres of land near Plains. Another, my final story of the summer, was an analysis of the cost of all the federal programs Carter had criticized Ford for vetoing. It was a varied but worthwhile few months in which to get to know the Carter organization better. But NBC News executives in New York had different ideas.

My last, best hope for the future, I thought, was to be assigned to cover Carter in the general election, and I figured that being the in-house expert on Carter might persuade my producers that I had the experience to handle the assignment. And so when Dick Fischer called to say, "We want our strongest people on the general election," and that I might be called upon from time to time to help out, I was crushed.

"Why?" I said. "I'm trying and I think I've done a good job."

"Your reporting has been fine," he said. "But this is the Big Time. It's the election of the President. Don't take it so hard."

"What do you mean your strongest people?" I said. "What's wrong with me. What am I doing wrong?"

"Judy, you need to work on your delivery. I've watched a couple of stories you've done recently, and you talk as though you were telling us about a ladies' tea party."

It seemed like the lowest point of my life. For eighteen months I had worked harder than I ever believed possible. For what? I thought about quitting NBC and going to work for a local station. I thought about quitting television altogether.

That week I went to dinner with Don Oliver. "Don't be so discouraged," he said. "People are up and down. It happens all the time. Don't forget, you've only been with the network a year and a half."

I took a two-week vacation to think it over. I weighed my options against the eight years that I had invested in the crazy business thus far. I realized that I had a lot more working for me than against me. Six years experience as a reporter, nearly two of those with a network, added up to something. I had learned so much; it would be a waste to throw it all away now. I decided that the best thing to do was to wait out the election. If nothing else, covering Carter's election bid as a third-string reporter would give me that all-prized experience everyone kept saying I lacked. Maybe third-string wasn't so bad after all.

That turned out to be the best advice I ever gave myself. During the general election campaign I had two short stints while Don Oliver and Kenley Jones took breathers. I was able to get several good stories on the air. On election night I was assigned to stake out Carter campaign headquarters and worked until four the next morning grabbing Carter people as they came in and out of the Omni hotel, getting their reactions as the votes came in. Over a six-week period when I was assigned to cover the transition after the election I broke the stories of the appointments of Andy Young as Ambassador to the United Nations, Griffin Bell as Attorney General and Juanita Kreps as Secretary of Commerce.

One afternoon in late December I was in the middle of putting together a piece for the "Nightly News" when I got a message to call Dick Fischer.

"We want to expand our team at the White House and add a third reporter," he said. "We want to send you."

Who You Know . . .

Compared with most reporters assigned to the White House, I am a newcomer to Washington. I arrived in the capital in January 1977, barely thirty years old and, like Jimmy Carter, an outsider from Georgia. I followed Carter from his early days as a national candidate to the most prestigious address and newsbeat in the world. I knew even less then about Washington and how it works than did the incoming members of the Carter Administration. And while I'd like to think that I caught on a little faster than they did, the only proof that I can offer is that I'm still here.

One fact about Washington became obvious very quickly, however: who you know can sometimes be almost as important as how much you know.

Making Washington contacts and cultivating them—a process crudely referred to as "stroking"—can be as easy as hanging a lamb chop in your window, which is how the late Marjorie Merriweather Post once described the secret of her success in gathering the big names of several Administrations around her dinner table. Or it can be as involved as the multi-million-dollar-a-year lobbying industry and its attendant weekly decathlon of benefits, receptions, and dinner parties regularly sponsored by corporations, trade associations, and anyone else eager to win friends and influence people in Washington.

But stroking is no more limited to lobbyists than to so-called social occasions. The methods and manner vary according to circumstances and who is stroking whom. When the President invites a senator or congressman to the Oval Office to seek his views or to ask for his help on a particular issue before the House or Senate, or when he invites a big campaign contributor to a White House dinner, that's stroking. And when a congressman, who is hoping that the hydroelectric dam in his district will be saved from the Administration's budget cuts, praises the President's economic plan in a speech, that's stroking, too.

Some of the most practiced strokers in town are reporters. A large portion of the stock-in-trade of any Washington journalist is a collection of sources, which is simply another name for contacts. Some of these sources are on the inside of power, some on the fringes, some are proven, some potential— but reporters cultivate all of them as carefully as cymbidium orchids.

Taking sources to breakfast or lunch is a daily ritual for many Washington reporters. Syndicated columnist Robert Novak, for example, breakfasts regularly with sources at the Hay Adams Hotel opposite Lafayette Square from the White House. Novak's more urbane partner, Rowland Evans, can be found most mornings dining with sources at the posh Metropolitan Club. There is always a free lunch awaiting any government official in Washington who is willing to be seen dining out with a reporter, which is why expense-account restaurants specializing in $15 steaks do a brisk business here. Although seldom does a front-page story or a lead piece on the evening network newscasts emerge over breakfast or lunch with a source, a reporter can glean pieces of stories, gossip, and insights across the table that can provide the context for interpreting news or information that emerges later. For the source, lunching with reporters can be a smart way to try to cultivate favor and develop off-the-record lines of communication that may be useful in the future.

Before coming to Washington I covered the Georgia state-house for an Atlanta television station and, later, everything from insect plagues to hurricanes for NBC's Atlanta bureau. On those assignments there was seldom time to cultivate sources. Covering a story generally meant little more than showing up with a television crew and firing off questions at the people I interviewed, most of whom were only too happy to talk. Except for occasionally grabbing a cup of coffee in some sandwich shop near the statehouse cafeteria, there was little opportunity for getting to know sources off the job, or for their getting to know me. Rarely did our social lives overlap.

But in Washington, I learned, social life and work are intertwined to the point that socializing is considered by some reporters to be as much a part of their jobs as filing stories. The dinner parties and receptions that make up political Washington's social life can provide reporters opportunities to meet and talk with people who won't return their telephone calls during the day. Over a couple of drinks in the relaxed atmosphere of a dinner party, sources will sometimes say things they would never say over the telephone.

For reporters the benefits of socializing with the people whom they cover are not without their price, however. Washington pays attention to those who have the President's ear and to those with entree to those who have the President's ear. Being able to say, "As Michael Deaver was telling me the other day. . ." can boost a reporter's status, even if it has no effect on the reporter's stories. But after a while the distinction between personal friends and professional sources can become uncomfortably blurred. Most reporters are invited to parties or intimate lunches because of their positions, not because of their wit and charm. The prudent reporter treasures his or her independent judgment more than entree to the powerful.

Even prudent reporters, however, make the common mistake of depending too much on personal contacts and not enough on documents and research. Because of our special deadline pressures, this is particularly true of those of us in television news. But it's a tendency for all reporters, mainly because it's often easier to get information from a source over the telephone than to dig it out from a government study or some other document. In his study *The Washington Reporters,* Stephen Hess found that even when newspaper and television reporters are given more time to do stories, "they simply do more interviews." As a result, we end up missing a lot because information may not be as complete or accurate when it's filtered through someone else. The biggest culprits, Hess says, are the White House television reporters, who use the fewest documents. To a large extent, he's right. Given the demands on our time and the energy we expend trying to get answers from the President and his men, the temptation is to rely too much on them for information in doing our research. But on the other hand, White House stories depend more than others on confidential information or insights, which can be gathered only through personal contact.

The longer I worked in Washington the more I came to see that the stereotype of how reporters deal with sources— cloak-and-dagger meetings in underground garages and midnight phone calls demanding to know the truth, the whole truth, and nothing but the truth—has more in common with Hollywood movies than with Washington reporting. Often the most ineffective way to get people to talk to you is to come at them head-on with an accusation. And getting people to talk to you is what reporting is all about, particularly if you are reporting on the White House, where your information so often depends on inside sources. Confrontation can be a useful technique in investigative reporting. But when you're covering a political or government beat day in and day out, there is more hard work than high drama in your job.

Stroking sources is done much the same way as cultivating business contacts: by staying in touch, gaining their trust, and establishing rapport. Instead of making the sale or securing the contract, however, the reporter's goal is obtaining information. As in business, there may be times when you must be a little disingenuous and cultivate sources you really don't much like personally. But if you are going to be able to rely on them for information, you must be pleasant and professional enough to reassure them that you will respect their confidences. On the other hand, there are sources whom you do come to like personally. And it can be difficult to walk that thin line between empathy and objectivity.

I think Washington reporters are given more credit and blame for being ruthless than they deserve. The temptation in this town is to be too soft on those we cover, not too tough. It's easy to become more concerned about offending than about reporting when the people you cover are so often the same people on whom you must rely for information. It's also far more difficult to come down hard on somebody in an interview or to ask the tough questions than I think the public realizes. My basic nature is that of someone who would like to be nice to people all of the time, probably because of my well-mannered, Southern upbringing. I'm uncomfortable acting tough and hard-nosed. But as with most competitive pursuits, nice reporters tend to finish last on the story. So, I've had to work to become more outspoken and assertive. I've also had to learn how to apply pressure and prod sources when I need to in order to get information. My natural tendency is to be understanding when a secretary tells me the boss is too busy to return my phone calls. But persistence, I've learned, is often the key to getting through.

Still, it's difficult for me to be tough. I don't relish that side of my job, or the stories that result in embarrassing or damaging someone else. But if I uncover a story that calls into question the integrity of a public official, I believe that I have an obligation to check it out. Fairness and accuracy are responsibilities I take seriously.

In the final weeks of the 1976 presidential campaign, while I was working in NBC's Atlanta bureau and helping to cover Jimmy Carter's campaign, I received a tip from a source that eventually led to the resignation of Earl Butz as Secretary of Agriculture under incumbent President Gerald Ford. In a widely circulated story published by *Rolling Stone* magazine, former Nixon White House counsel John Dean had recounted a conversation he had overheard between singer Pat Boone and an unnamed Cabinet officer aboard a plane returning from the Republican National Convention. According to Dean, Boone asked why the Republican Party could not attract more black voters, and the Cabinet officer replied: "Because colored only want three things . . . first, a tight (woman's sexual organ); second, loose shoes; and third, a warm place to (defecate)." My source, who was a journalist, told me that another magazine, *New Times,* was about to identify Butz as the one who had made the tasteless remark.

That a top Administration official demonstrated such an astonishing lack of discretion and sensitivity made this a valid news story. But the incident was also political dynamite with the election just four weeks off. As an ambitious young reporter, I was pleased to have such a potentially explosive tip. But I was nervous about confronting Butz with the remark in order to give him the chance to deny or explain it. I telephoned Butz's office and was told by a Department of Agriculture spokesman that the Secretary could not be reached. Next I phoned the White House press secretary, Ron Nessen. I informed Nessen matter-of-factly that I was checking out a report, and told him of the remark Butz had allegedly made.

After several long seconds, Nessen finally responded. "Aren't you really close with the Carter people?" he asked, clearly implying that I was pursuing the story to help Jimmy Carter.

I had expected Nessen to try to discredit the story, but I wasn't prepared for his attempt to discredit me. I was stung by Nessen's remark, although I should have known that he was trying to throw me off guard. Still, it was disappointing that Nessen, who had worked as a reporter for NBC before joining the Ford Administration, didn't appreciate that we both had jobs to do. Trying to hide my trepidation, I pressed him for an official reaction from the White House. Instead of confirming or denying the incident, Nessen kept trying to get me to tell him whether I intended to go with the story even if I couldn't get a reaction from the White House. That's when I began to suspect that the story was true and that confirming it was simply a matter of beating the clock.

To put pressure on Nessen, I told him I was probably going with the story with or without a reaction from him. He said he would call me back with a comment after checking with Butz. I waited, as my deadline approached, knowing that without a reaction from the White House or Butz I probably had no story. Nessen never did call *me* back. Instead, he phoned the "Nightly News" producer in New York fifteen minutes before the newscast went on the air, and dictated a terse statement. Anchorman John Chancellor reported that President Ford and the White House deeply regretted the remarks made by Butz and that Butz had offered his resignation. Ford later accepted it.

There aren't many reporters prospering in Washington who are sloppy with facts, or who don't carefully utilize sources.

The two-source rule was popularized during Watergate. Bob Woodward and Carl Bernstein, the *Washington Post* reporters who broke that story, claimed they never went into print without at least two sources. Most journalists, however, don't quantify the number of sources necessary to go with a story. What counts is the reliability and knowledge of your source or sources. I have broadcast stories, which I either broke or advanced, based on one source who I was convinced was credible and informed. Sometimes, however, a story is of such magnitude that it must be verified, even if it has come from an unimpeachable source. Alas, that's the way we lose some pretty good stories—as I found out six months into the Carter Administration.

Washington had been waiting anxiously for President Carter's first major strategic defense decision—whether he would go ahead with production of the B-1 bomber—when an Administration source I trusted gave me advance word. He told me that the President had decided not to build the B-1 and would announce his decision within the next day or two. Because the story was so important, I made phone calls to several members of the very top Carter senior staff to ask for confirmation. As it turned out, the only one I could reach was Hamilton Jordan, who assured me that no decision had been reached and added that it would be a mistake to go with the report. Because of Jordan's response, I didn't run with the story. The next day, Carter announced just what I had been told—that he would not go ahead with the B-1. Jordan had lied to keep the President's announcement from being preempted. His behavior took me by surprise and changed my impression of him. I never again believed anything he told me.

I know that several important people in the Carter Administration, including White House Chief of Staff Jordan, arrived in Washington suspecting the worst motives from the Washington press corps. Recognizing this, a few reporters who knew the Carter people from the campaign started inviting them to a Washington bar near the White House called the "Class Reunion." Known as a political hangout where Republicans and Democrats drank at opposite ends of the bar and reporters, presumably free of such biases, played the two sides off against each other, the "Class Reunion" was regarded by regulars, somewhat loftily, as the Speakers' Corner of American political debate. Besides reporters, those regulars were political staffers from the Hill and the current Administration, lobbyists, political consultants, and Republican and Democratic Party operatives. A few shared beers have a way of making unlikely friends, which is probably why the tenor of those political discussions was usually good-natured chiding.

My own view is that the value for journalists of these social sessions, or drinking bouts, can be frequently exaggerated. No doubt spending time with a source in an informal atmosphere can break down barriers, perhaps leading to a better understanding of the people and policies we are covering. Conversely, the Carter Administration would have profited if more of the Georgians had spent time at cocktail parties, ballgames, and bars with Washington insiders. But most good journalists realize that such socializing is no substitute for reading dreary documents, making countless calls, or talking to especially sober bureaucrats. Usually, this isn't as much fun. But this sort of routine often produces more good stories and insights than many of the most glittering Georgetown dinner parties.

Still, I probably missed out by not joining the "Class Reunion" scene, but I've never made a habit of drinks after work. I don't have any moral objections to the practice; it's just that a couple of glasses of wine put me to sleep. Of course, I've passed my share of evenings comparing notes over drinks with other reporters and White House aides while covering the President on the road. But I've often paid a head-splitting price for it the next day. It's just not part of my constitution or style, which seems to be true of most women. And that just may be one of the handicaps we have in trying to do our jobs in a largely male world. We don't exploit the kinds of natural icebreakers that our male colleagues can rely on to establish that crucial camaraderie, whether it's playing golf with the boss or drinking with political and business contacts. But while it's a problem women share, I don't think it's an insurmountable one, at least not in my profession. I've seen enough ginger ale-sipping women reporters close as many bars on the campaign trail as their hard-drinking male counterparts.

What all Washington reporters discover is that there are some sources in this town who are too busy to make time to have lunch and unable to talk over the telephone during the day. Sometimes after work is the only time they are willing or able to meet. But this can create complications. A few weeks after I began covering the Carter presidency, I arranged to have dinner with an Administration official who worked outside the White House. I had known this man in Atlanta before the election and found him to be direct and well-plugged-in to the Carter inner circle. When he was appointed to a top department post, I saw him as a valuable potential source. He suggested a dimly lit restaurant near his apartment in northwest Washington. I thought it was an odd choice of meeting places, but certainly no more odd than those underground garage meetings between "Deep Throat" and Bob Woodward during Watergate. I figured my source was worried about being seen with a reporter.

My reservations about the restaurant were quickly assuaged, however, by his remarkable candor in criticizing the Carter White House for bungling some important decisions affecting his department. I listened closely. And when he invited me up for a drink, I accepted because I was eager to hear more. Much of what he had to say was new to me.

So was his next move. Once inside the apartment, he had

barely taken a sip of his bourbon and water when he lunged at me from across the sofa. "I think I'd better go," I said, springing from the couch.

From then on, I limited my few contacts with him to the telephone.

Although this Mad Masher and Deep Throat shared a flair for adventurous meetings, they are the exception when it comes to Washington sources. The sources I've come to know are straight-laced, briefcase-toting, play-by-the-rules types who work as mid-level bureaucrats, congressional staffers, and White House aides. In persuading them to talk, simple persistence is generally more useful than a free lunch, because they often don't have time to eat. I called one mid-level White House source five times a day for five weeks to talk about Reagan's economic program before he finally began sporadically returning my calls. It has taken him months to learn that he can trust me to protect his anonymity.

Most sources cross the threshold from silent witness to helpful informant for one of three reasons: to advance themselves and their cause; to seek revenge against or to damage the political opposition; or to provide an outlet for frustrated idealism.

At the White House, sources' motives are less diverse than, say, in Congress. Their overriding goal is to further the policies and political standing of the President. (Many aides don't think it's worth talking to the press at all, and, as a rule, mid-level aides talk more—and more candidly—than their superiors. Of course, they usually don't know as much.) Many White House staffers give you what is little more than press agentry: "The President is a very tough decision maker in times like this." Or, "The old man has incredible knowledge on this subject."

In his insightful book, *Robert Pierpoint at the White House,* the CBS correspondent recalls an important insider's tip during the height of Watergate. Long after Nixon's chief of staff, H. R. Haldeman, had been dismissed, Pierpoint learned that he was still in frequent contact with top White House officials, including the President. The resulting story hurt Nixon, who was trying to give the impression of having weeded out those advisers tainted by the scandal. But it was apparently leaked by someone on Nixon's staff who believed the President would benefit by terminating his relationship with Haldeman.

Unlike their counterparts in other areas of government, White House sources rarely disagree with the President. They know that if he looks good, they look good. They may offer some insignificant criticism of him, such as "The old man really blew that one," after an obvious Presidential mistake. (The message to me, they hope, is that they can be trusted and are really candid.) But they will rarely express serious disagreement with Presidential decisions. Even after one of those coy moments of candor, they often come back to emphasize what a wonderful job the President is doing on everything else. Reluctance to criticize the President doesn't stem just from feelings of loyalty, however. White House officials frequently trade information on which reporters they've talked with. I'm no longer surprised when a White House aide knowingly says to me, "Oh well, you've just talked to [another White House aide], haven't you?"

The goal of furthering the stature of the President also means that White House aides are expected to remain in the background—literally as well as figuratively. Rarely do the President's men speak on the record for attribution, even when the information they are providing has been approved by the President. Consequently, many stories that appear to have originated through confidential White House sources and enterprising reporting are actually the product of White House background briefings. These are sessions in which the White House press secretary, or some other top aide, invites a hand-picked group of reporters to discuss a subject in more detail than the daily press-briefing may permit. Because the official conducting the briefing sets the ground rules, reporters agree in advance to use only a vague attribution, such as "an administration official," in describing their source. Some briefings, usually on national security matters, are conducted on a *deep* background basis, meaning that an even vaguer attribution must be used, such as "It is understood that the President is considering. . . ."

Before I began covering the White House, I had never heard of deep background, nor had I ever seen supposedly confidential sources doling out information to groups of reporters like some college professor. It didn't occur to me that I was expected to protect the identity of the briefer—even from other reporters who had not attended the briefing. To me, background briefings seemed the worst-kept secrets in the White House press room, since even those who were excluded often knew when a briefing was scheduled and who was conducting it. So, when I walked out of one deep backgrounder with Carter national security assistant Zbigniew Brzezinski, and UPI correspondent Helen Thomas asked me what Brzezinski had said, I told her. Since Helen had not participated in the briefing, she was not bound by any of the ground rules. So she filed her story referring to Brzezinski by name as the source of her information. Within an hour Brzezinski's press spokesman, Gerald Schecter, discovered that I had spilled the beans. "You're not supposed to be sharing deep background briefings with other reporters," he said indignantly, as though I had violated a secret oath.

"Why not?" I asked. "You told me."

He explained that wire-service reporters are deliberately excluded from such backgrounders because it is difficult for them to use information not attributed to a particular source. As ludicrous as trying to keep a secret among a dozen reporters seemed to me, I promised Schecter that my lips would be sealed from then on. Later, I learned that Brzezinski stayed angry with me over the incident for weeks.

The information dispensed at these backgrounders is handed out only after careful consideration of where and when it will do the President and the White House the most good. Besides promoting the President and his policies, they are sometimes a way of manipulating reporters and the news, which is why reporters should not accept the information they are given without checking with sources with a different point of view. Unfortunately, that's not always possible.

Briefings are sometimes used by the White House to give reporters with influential news organizations the inside track on a presidential decision. When President Reagan was preparing to announce economic sanctions against the Soviets as a reprisal for the declaration of martial law in Poland, a few reporters were given the word in advance. White House officials evidently figured that network reporters' speculating about how tough the steps would be would leave less room for pointing out, after they were announced, that the President's response contained more symbolism than substance. Alternatively, briefings may be a way to use reporters to reach certain audiences first. If the White House wants to reach the business community, they invite the *Wall Street Journal* and the *New York Times;* if they want to reach Mr. and Mrs. Front Porch America, they invite the networks.

Besides controlling who attends briefings, White House officials carefully time the release of the information they give out. Often, briefings are deliberately scheduled late in the day, leaving little time for reporters to research interpretations outside the White House and still meet their deadlines. In one late-afternoon briefing on Carter's decision not to deploy the neutron weapon in Europe, we were told by Press Secretary Jody Powell and Brzezinski that this was not a final decision and that there was a good chance the President would change his mind later. With my deadline rapidly approaching, I took Brzezinski and Powell at their word and reported that Carter's decision could change later—remembering, of course, not to mention any names. Several days later, after talking to sources outside the White House, I realized that my report had played right into the hands of the Carter Administration, which was trying to appease both sides by making the announcement appear more tentative than it was. By announcing that the bomb would not be deployed, the Carterites could quiet the growing antinuclear movement in the Western European countries which were slated to serve as deployment sites. By intimating that the decision was not a final one, the Administration could temporarily assuage European leaders, who were looking for the President to take the lead on deployment, and congressional hawks, who were concerned that giving up the weapon would weaken U.S. defenses. And by briefing reporters on a background basis, Powell and Brzezinski could be sure that neither they nor the Administration would be held accountable for what they were putting out if they didn't wish. I took them at their word, and looked foolish as a result.

Another way White House sources use reporters is by planting stories which they hope will send a message to Congress, an executive department, a foreign power, or sometimes even the President himself. Among White House policy advisers who are responsible for shepherding individual issues, there is often as much jockeying for the President's attention as for his favor. Leaking information to reporters is a ploy frequently used by White House aides to call the President's attention to a problem or to test his commitment to a particular issue. Sometimes a reporter, whether through a news story or a question to the President during a news conference or photo opportunity, can prompt the President to focus on or commit publicly to an issue he has previously overlooked or ignored.

Releasing a story that the President is considering such and such a move is also a way for White House sources to test domestic political waters, or to send a diplomatic warning that could be construed as a threat if issued directly by the White House, or sometimes just to blow smoke. Whatever the reason for talking, White House aides almost always stress that they wish to remain anonymous. But even when they don't, it's supposed to be understood. I learned that when I quoted Zbigniew Brzezinski's deputy by name in a story.

Following an appearance by Brzezinski on NBC's "Meet the Press" in which he revealed that there was evidence of possible Soviet involvement in Zaire, I phoned his deputy, David Aaron, whom I had not been able to get to very often before. But on this Sunday morning I found Aaron exceptionally willing to talk. Not only did he discuss Brzezinski's revelation about the Soviets in detail, but he volunteered that the President was thinking about taking some action against Cuba, possibly curtailing American tourism, in retaliation for Cuban involvement in Zaire. That night, I dutifully quoted Aaron as saying that the President was considering sanctions against Cuba. The next day, Aaron was on the phone to me, furious because I had used his name in my story. I never said I wouldn't and he never asked me not to. Nevertheless, I was *supposed* to know. And as a result of mentioning Aaron's name, I lost a potentially good source. After that, I found him even more difficult to reach than before.

The Reagan Administration is more skilled than its predecessor at using the news media to promote its policies. During consideration in the Senate of the controversial proposal to sell sophisticated radar planes to Saudi Arabia, the White House carefully orchestrated commitments, spaced a day or two apart, from more than a dozen Republican Senators. It really wasn't news that these Reagan loyalists—Utah's Orrin Hatch, Wyoming's Alan Simpson, or Indiana's Dan Quayle—were backing the President on this issue. But White House sources carefully put out the word in advance and managed to create a sense of minor momentum in the President's direction. This, no doubt, was a factor in the narrow fifty-two to forty-eight approval by the Senate of the sale in late October 1981. We were used—effectively.

Nevertheless, good, straightforward sources can be developed at the White House. But it takes work. More phone calls have to be made, more stroking has to be done, and more trust has to be developed. One asset we have going for us in developing key sources within the White House is that rival camps and power struggles inevitably emerge in any Administration. The one camp is quite willing to discuss the shortcomings or even question the integrity of the other, though reporters have to be wary of exaggeration in these instances.

The feud in the Reagan White House between former national security assistant Richard Allen and Secretary of State Alexander Haig was a good example. For a time, word circulated and was reported—quoting unnamed sources, of course—that Haig's conflicts with Allen were casting serious doubts on his longevity as Secretary of State. At one point, the President placed a call to columnist Jack Anderson to refute the story. Meanwhile, other White House sources intimated that Richard Allen wasn't performing his job competently. On the heels of that, word leaked out that Allen had accepted a cash "honorarium" from a Japanese magazine on behalf of Mrs. Reagan, money which he had failed to turn over to the proper authorities. After the story about Allen's acceptance of the cash was out, the FBI began an investigation. Even though the Bureau ultimately cleared him of any criminal wrongdoing, Allen's fate had been sealed, and White House aides were tripping over each other to give reporters damaging information about him.

More often, however, White House sources tend to cast doubts on, or discuss the shortcomings of, rivals on the outside. Attacking the integrity of a political adversary is the easiest way to discredit him. In few other towns do reputations matter so much. A Cleveland insurance broker who has shady friends or overdraws his bank account may find himself the subject of gossip. But a public official who does the same things can become the subject of a government investigation—and end up out of a job. Because public officials are sworn to uphold the public trust, they are expected to be above reproach. Their private lives, personal finances, and previous peccadilloes cease to be private matters, particularly if any hint of scandal is involved.

You would think that the people who live in such glass houses would be loath to throw stones. But in Washington the opposite is true. What is considered slander in most towns is considered simply an occupational hazard here. Among Washington sources mudslinging is almost as common as self-promotion. Like promoters, mudslingers usually stand to gain directly or indirectly from the damaging information they pass on to reporters. They may be seeking revenge for an attack against them or their bosses, or attempting to discredit a political opponent, or seizing an opportunity to "do in" a rival who stands in their way. Sometimes they offer little more than suggestions ("You ought to look into . . ."). Occasionally they provide proof to support their allegations. No prudent reporter accepts hearsay as fact from such obviously biased sources. And yet, no good reporter can afford to ignore information simply because his source has an axe to grind. A reporter's job is to listen to all kinds of sources with all kinds of tips.

In the Nixon White House leaking information damaging to political opponents was done so systematically that the job was delegated to Special Counsel to the President Charles Colson, who headed what was referred to as the dirty tricks department. Once, Colson tried to use my husband, who was then covering economics for the *Wall Street Journal.* He had one of the Administration's press aides call Al to reveal that Nixon was "furious" with Arthur Burns, who was then chairman of the Federal Reserve Board, and to say that the President was giving "serious consideration" to asking Congress to bring the independent Board into the executive branch. Colson told Al that while Burns was calling for anti-inflationary steps he "hypocritically" was secretly lobbying for a pay raise for himself. Al knew, however, that the independent-minded Burns was becoming a political thorn in the side of the Nixon White House. And he suspected that the Administration had decided that a carefully placed, damaging leak might cause Burns to keep quiet. So, instead of writing a straight account of the "background information" he had been given by Colson, Al wrote an account of the "escalating war of nerves" between the White House and the Federal Reserve Board and the methods the Nixonites were using to try to silence Arthur Burns.

Generally, the Carter and Reagan Administrations have not been as heavy-handed as the infamous Chuck Colson and the Nixon group. But one of the more blatant examples of a Carter White House source leaking information was intended to damage a political opponent. During the Bert Lance banking scandal, Jody Powell suggested to several reporters—I was not one of them—that they ought to check out Senator Charles Percy's personal use of corporate planes. At the time, Percy was the ranking Republican member of the Senate Banking Committee, which was overseeing the congressional investigation into Lance's financial dealings at the Calhoun National Bank in Georgia. When reporters were unable to produce any evidence of wrongdoing on Percy's part, Loye Miller of the

Chicago Sun-Times decided to report instead on Powell's attempt to discredit Percy. Powell's move backfired and ended up damaging him and the President.

Although they tend to be the most honest sources, frustrated idealists are also the most reluctant. They see themselves as public servants with an obligation to the public good, or at least to their interpretation of it. But they are frequently torn between a sense of responsibility to the public and loyalty to their superiors. One of my best sources in the Carter Administration started out believing that Jimmy Carter had many of the right answers. But when Carter made several political concessions on key issues about which the source felt strongly, he became increasingly disenchanted with the President's lack of resolve. Eventually, he grew so unhappy that he left the Administration. But in the months before his departure he wrestled with his conscience on the telephone with me, reluctant to criticize the President even though he felt betrayed by him.

Some mid-level Carter aides were genuinely upset about the ineptitude at the top level. They would sometimes leak stories about the latest miscue by Carter Chief of Staff Hamilton Jordan or congressional liaison Frank Moore. For several of these sources, I think the motive was a sincere desire to see the Administration get its act together and govern better. Similarly, some reasonably high level Reagan aides were quick to tell tales about the inadequacy of former national security assistant Richard Allen and the disorganization of White House counselor Edwin Meese because they genuinely wanted to see operations improved.

Some of the most overlooked sources in Washington are other journalists. Many reporters bounce ideas off each other, trade information, and speculate about political fortunes. Some of this is inevitable; almost any group is influenced to an extent by its professional peers. But government officials sometimes

My cramped press office at the White House. On the bulletin board are printed schedules of the President's daily appearances, which I must attend. Much of my time here is spent on the phone and at the typewriter. (Barbara Ries)

Summer 1976, after a softball game in Plains, Georgia. Democratic nominee for President (and pitcher) Carter poses with his press teammates. (Women were later excluded from these press-staff games.)

The two newcomers to the White House: President Carter's first week in Washington—and mine too. (White House Photo)

Vying with other Washington correspondents for former President Carter's attention at a White House press conference. Being heard in these circumstances is usually a matter of who's the fastest and the loudest. (White House Photo)

Returning to Washington on the press plane from former President Carter's summit meeting with Allied heads of state in Guadeloupe (1/9/79). A chance to relax and clown around with correspondents (left to right): Bob Schieffer (CBS News), Sam Donaldson (ABC News), Ann Compton (ABC News), me, Bob Pierpoint (CBS News), and Lee Thornton (then with CBS News).

Jostling with other White House reporters for answers from Sen. John Danforth (R., Missouri). (Barbara Ries)

Al and me with Jeffrey, age five months. (Diana Walker/Time)

A light moment at the White House—President Reagan makes friends with Jeffrey, whom we encourage to be a bi-partisan baby. (White House Photo)

An animated President Reagan illustrates a point to me and colleagues Sam Donaldson and Lesley Stahl. (White House Photo)

complain that reporters listen to each other too much, especially during political campaigns, and that pack journalism results. They may have a point. Although it's natural that people who work in the same profession compare notes, we probably tend to reinforce each other's ideas and opinions too much, even if inadvertently.

A correlative problem is that we may rely too much on each other's broadcasts and clips. My friend Mark Shields, a columnist for the *Washington Post,* talks about the "first clip" syndrome of American politics. Namely, the first clip about a politician or issue is often the most important because it immediately goes to the top of every other reporter's clip file on that subject, and thus sets the tone for subsequent stories.

We owe it to ourselves and to the audience whom we ask to believe us to cultivate the widest range of sources in our pursuit of information. Reliance on too few sources is a concern that extends beyond journalistic incestuousness. It's just as dangerous for reporters to rely too much on official government sources and the information they hand out. Naturally, not many government officials see this as a problem.

The most serious dilemma for journalists, however, is striking the right balance in reliance on and relationships with sources. In a city that often seems like a small village, social contact with both sources and people we are reporting on is unavoidable. Moreover, there are some sources and some politicians whom we see fairly frequently. That, of course, raises the question of whether you can be tough, in a news sense, with someone you had dinner with the night before. The only answer is that if you can't you shouldn't be writing or broadcasting about that person. It would be naive to suggest that human feelings don't affect journalists. But in the crunch, it's a disservice to our viewers or readers to allow personal considerations to overshadow professional responsibilities. I was personally fond of Jimmy Carter's embattled budget director, Bert Lance, and his wife, Labelle. But that didn't deter me from covering Lance's travails, a professional responsibility which I doubt Mrs. Lance ever understood.

Balance also is necessary in our attitudes towards what sources are telling us. Watergate and Vietnam taught us that a healthy dose of skepticism is essential for a journalist. We should prod, push, insist, demand—even behave obnoxiously at times—to get information and serve the public's right to know. Yet we shouldn't resort to such cheap cynicism that we believe little we are told or see a dark ulterior motive behind every word and deed.

Moreover, we need to strike a sense of balance in the use of confidential sources. Obviously, there are many times it is necessary to rely on a "source" who cannot be identified for very legitimate reasons, such as that his position might be jeopardized. Further, many people talk much more candidly with the protection of anonymity. These "well-placed" or "informed," but unnamed, sources are important to gathering accurate information on government. But the opportunities for abuse are frightening. Anonymous sources can attack, discredit, and impugn others with little fear of accountability. Thus, we must be very careful and selective in using confidential sources for edification and education and not for any form of character assassination.

In retrospect, there are times I wish I had been more alert to such abuses. For instance, when Reagan's national security assistant, Richard Allen, was on his way out, I think I wrongly permitted some White House aides to make some gratuitous criticisms of him, under the protection of anonymity.

Obviously, we all seek a multiplicity of diverse sources. In the final analysis, though, even more important than the quality of sources is our own instinct. I think this was put best some years ago by *New York Times* columnist Tom Wicker. In his book *On Press,* he wrote: "My experience has been . . . (that) an independent and courageous reporter can almost always get whatever information he or she needs on adequate ethical terms, without paying too high a price in advantage to the source or in restraint on himself or herself. If sources do not want to "deal" on that basis, the reporter can do surprisingly well without them.

"Sometimes—usually, I'd say—instinct, experience, a good memory, a sharp eye, careful attention to surrounding detail, a skeptical sense of the way things work, a wary regard for human nature yield far more useful information and insights than any number of self-serving news sources and official spokesmen."

Two Presidents: Two Images

No two successive Presidents in recent history have been more contrasting in character, temperament, and style than the two I have covered in the White House. James Earl Carter and Ronald Wilson Reagan are as different in demeanor as Plains and Hollywood. One might have to go back as far as the patrician John Quincy Adams and the populist Andrew Jackson to find two successive chief executives as different in personality and character as Carter and Reagan.

Jimmy Carter is one of the brightest men I have ever met. He possesses a disciplined mind, a tough, determined nature, and a boundless, aggressive desire to achieve his goals. He combines eclectic interests with a first-class intellect; he is equally proficient in talking about nuclear physics and country music. Paradoxically, this immensely bright man also has a surprising streak of insecurity. Generally, he was loath to surround himself with people as bright or as educated as he was, preferring intimates who were either much younger or plainly his intellectual inferiors. Ten years ago I remember one of the few pro-Carter lawmakers in the Georgia state legislature noting that then-Governor Jimmy Carter hated to spend much time around people who were more knowledgeable than he about a subject.

In sharp contrast to this insecurity was what came through to many people as an attitude of supreme self-confidence, and even moral superiority. Adding to the contradiction was, despite the morality Carter preached, a streak of petty meanness which appeared at critical times in his campaigns and his presidency. As surprising as it was initially to find these traits so strongly represented in one person, on reflection they don't seem so mutually exclusive.

Moreover, to continue this contradictory picture, Jimmy Carter's absorptive mind produced a fastidious attention to detail that sometimes precluded him from establishing priorities, a prerequisite for addressing broader philosophical questions. In particular, he never seemed able to convey where he wanted to lead the country.

Ronald Reagan is about 170 degrees from this portrait. He is bright, but even his most ardent supporters would be hard-pressed to argue that Reagan is as intelligent or as disciplined as his predecessor. Longtime Reagan observer and biographer Lou Cannon of the *Washington Post* theorizes that Reagan has a near photographic memory, and that this permitted him to develop uneven work habits, starting in college. Now, fifty years later, there are times that those work habits border on the indolent, and all too frequently he appears oblivious to or uninterested in the important details of state. But he is also a man of considerable confidence who is comfortable in delegating details to a pretty impressive and experienced group of advisers. If he is weak on details, there is little doubt that Ronald Reagan has a good idea of what he wants to do and where he wants to lead.

The distinctions are equally sharp in the way these two men viewed the press. Before the 1976 presidential campaign, Jimmy Carter spent considerable time deciding how to cultivate members of the national press. He would go to great lengths to see key reporters and show off his political and intellectual wares. But this was a chore, and his success was a testament not to Carter's charm but to his dogged determination. For he had little regard for most reporters, either personally or professionally. Thus, in the end, Carters' stroking of journalists fell flat. Even earlier, some of the more prescient members of the press saw the flaws. "The more I see Carter, the more I wonder about his kind of behavior," James Perry wrote in the *National Observer* in 1976. "He is a very tough fellow, he seems to nurse grudges, and he tends to lash out at people who criticize him, even when their intentions are honorable."

Ronald Reagan, by contrast, is a man of genuine charm who likes a lot of reporters and enjoys bantering with them. He has always had trouble with the notion of his conservative brethren that the press was the enemy. He even possesses real affection for some reporters who write tough but fair critiques of his performance. (At the top of this list is the granddaddy of Reagan watchers, Lou Cannon.)

While Carter's coldness and Reagan's charm affected how they were regarded by reporters, the press strategies of these two Presidents were as different from their public images as the two men were from each other.

Calculating and remote Jimmy Carter presided over one of the most open and accessible Administrations since the advent of daily White House press coverage. He viewed the press as his enemy and complained about unduly rough treatment by the media, but he didn't shrink from reporters. Carter averaged two nationally televised news conferences a month during his first year in office. In casual encounters with reporters his end of the conversation often seemed forced, and Carter seemed uneasy. But in news conferences and interviews he demonstrated his ability to hold his own. Carter's command of detail made him an effective advocate for himself and his Administration in these situations. And yet, by the end of his term, Carter's image was one of ineptitude, an image he blamed largely on the press. He was so embittered toward the news media that he banned TV cameras from his last two news conferences and vowed to continue the policy if reelected.

The seemingly forthcoming and frank Ronald Reagan presides over the most tightly controlled flow of information from the White House since the days of Richard Nixon. Although he appears comfortable with reporters, he is the first President with any long-term broadcast experience, and has been dubbed "The Great Communicator," Reagan held only seven televised press conferences in his entire first year in office—none of them during prime time.

While Carter was free to make a point during a photo opportunity and to stop and answer questions during those ritual gatherings of reporters, Reagan's appearances before the press are closely guarded by his staff for fear that his lack of knowledge about specifics and his penchant for telling anecdotal stories will get him into trouble. With Reagan, when we gather on the South Lawn to witness *Marine One*'s departure, the helicopter's loud engines are often started as soon as the President appears, drowning out our questions. During photo opportunities and impromptu situations where we are close enough to be heard, reporters' questions to Reagan are often greeted with the cry of "Lights!" (a signal to turn them out), gestures by nervous aides, or their shouts of "No interviews!" Once, when I posed a question about MX missile deployment during a photo opportunity, the President was interrupted by his counsellor, Ed Meese, before he could get a word out. "Mr. President, you know you don't have to answer that," Meese interjected.

The backdrop of press-presidential relations is important in understanding the attitudes of both men here. While an unavoidably adversarial relationship between the press and the President has existed since the days of George Washington, its intensity ebbs and flows. Contrary to popular belief, the press isn't populated by a bunch of biased left-wing ideologues; most of us are amazingly nonideological. Instead, as Haynes Johnson, the distinguished journalist, wrote in his book on the Carter years, *In the Absence of Power;* "If anything, the press is biased toward the system, suspicious of the new, distrustful of the maverick, comfortable with the conventional." Yet, as Johnson notes elsewhere, these relations reached poisonous proportions by the mid-1970s: "The legacy of Vietnam and Watergate was destructive: a near venomous state of relations between the press and the foreign policy and executive establishment [existed]. . . . In the Vietnam-Watergate years, the press learned it had allowed itself to be used by presidents." Thus, the many negative legacies that Richard Nixon bequeathed us included an even greater-than-usual mistrust and cynicism on the part of the press toward politicians in general and Presidents in particular.

Why then has Ronald Reagan managed so much better in this environment than Jimmy Carter? Part of the answer, no doubt, is luck and timing. Politicians, like generals, often fight the last war. As the Carter public relations aide, Greg Schneiders, told me, Carter's press relations, like much of his presidency, "was a reaction against the excesses of the Nixon Administration." Carter was open and accessible, not because that was a well-planned strategy or the one the participants were most comfortable with, but because that was what Richard Nixon was not. This was hardly an advantageous style for a man who basically didn't consider reporters very serious people and whose top staff, with notable exceptions like Greg Schneiders and Jody Powell, were almost equally contemptuous of the press. "Carter felt that most of the press didn't share his view of sound policies. . . . They only were interested in exploiting conflict and in having a 'good story,'" Schneiders notes.

The Reaganites, by contrast, were extremely well prepared to take advantage of their predecessors' mistakes. For one thing, Reagan probably has a better understanding of both the press and how to play it than did Carter. "Unlike Nixon, Reagan has a very good attitude about the press," suggests

John Sears, one of the most prominent Republican strategist in the country and a man who worked for both Presidents. "Reagan was more spontaneous and at ease with the press. He basically understood why the press behaved as it did. Don't forget he came from a background (the entertainment industry) where the press was vital." In addition, Reagan's experience as Governor for eight years, dealing with a skeptical California press corps, probably helped to prepare him for the Washington news media."

Even the sorts of problems that plagued the two men as candidates seemed to give Reagan the edge. Carter's problems were ones of personal character: the meanness issue. This was the man who in 1980 seemed to suggest that if Jimmy Carter weren't reelected, racial and religious and regional strife would break out all over the country, and thermonuclear war might start abroad. "Just as surely as the werewolf grows long fangs and facial hair on a full moon, the darker side of President Carter emerges in election years," longtime Carter watcher Curtis Wilkie wrote in the *Boston Globe.* Carter campaigns are "the symbol of gracelessness under pressure," Wilkie added.

Reagan's problem was gaffes: the man shot from the hip and often got his facts wrong. This was the candidate who called the Vietnam War a "noble cause," and who mistakenly accused Carter of opening his campaign in the "city that gave birth to and is the parent body of the Ku Klux Klan." In their book *Blue Smoke and Mirrors,* political writers Jack Germond and Jules Witcover note Reagan's penchant for uncritically reading claims and then simply repeating them. As a result, at one point top aide Michael Deaver actually hid copies of the conservative weekly *Human Events* so that Reagan wouldn't be able to read it.

While Reagan's perceived problem—questionable intellectual depth—might appear more serious to some, it actually was accorded less weight among many members of the press than the perceived character weaknesses of Carter. Reporters, believe it or not, harbor the same human feelings as most of the rest of the public. And the fact that Ronald Reagan was a much more likable figure than Jimmy Carter plainly helped him. For as the *Washington Post*'s Lou Cannon notes, Reagan "basically is a friendly guy. In fact, he believes if he had you or me sitting down one-on-one with him, he could convince us that his ideas are the best ones."

To be sure, Reagan's performance in office in the beginning of his term probably played the most important role in his generally more favorable news treatment. In his first year in office Reagan dazzled the Congress and the public with his remarkable presence during the assassination attempt, pushed through the most sweeping budget cutbacks and tax cuts in decades, and snatched victory from the jaws of defeat in winning Senate acceptance of a sale of radar planes to Saudi Arabia.

By contrast, after his first year in office Carter's major initiative, energy legislation, was hopelessly bogged down, congressional members of his own party were increasingly critical of their leader, and his own White House staff seemed in disarray.

For better or worse, there is some sports writer in most political journalists. And in the won-lost column Ronald Reagan had a much more impressive debut than his predecessor. Moreover, Reagan handled his crises better. Carter really started to slip in public esteem, according to pollsters, during the ill-fated Bert Lance affair in August, 1977. Lance's overdrafts at Georgia's Calhoun National Bank certainly was a serious issue, especially when it involved the federal government's top budget officer. The press eagerly moved to seize upon this new Administration's vulnerability, producing some exaggerated and even incorrect accounts. Yet Jimmy Carter's stubbornness in sticking by his close friend, and then a few days later having to let him go, hardly engendered confidence in the President's competence. By comparison, Ronald Reagan displayed little of that vacillation in sacrificing his national security chief, Richard Allen, after Allen was accused of improperly receiving favors from the Japanese—though Allen, of course, wasn't a close friend of the President's, as Lance was.

Still, if there were legitimate reasons for Reagan's better press treatment, we should also admit that the Reagan merchandising effort often overwhelmed us. This Administration came to town determined to totally control and manipulate the news agenda, and from Jim Baker and Michael Deaver on down this effort was concerted and calculating. Reagan brought into the White House some of the most sophisticated and skillful pollsters, media strategists, and tacticians ever to work at 1600 Pennsylvania Avenue. Under the direction of political poll taker Richard Wirthlin, the new team immediately molded a strategy for an auspicious start. It was entitled "The First 90 Days Project." David Gergen, former editor of *Public Opinion* magazine, was put in charge of the plan. A former White House speech writer under Nixon and Ford, Gergen was a savvy media mastermind in his own right. He was the one who suggested that candidate Reagan end the debate with Carter with the question that haunted the incumbent for the remainder of the campaign: "Are you better off now than you were four years ago?"

Gergen rechristened the plan "The First 100 Days," and set to work compiling all the events of the first 100 days of every president since Franklin D. Roosevelt. "We drew three conclusions," Gergen told writer Sidney Blumenthal in a *New York Times Magazine* article on the marketing of Ronald Reagan. "One, the first 100 days is the time during which the President establishes his Presidential persona. Two, the general character of the Administration is established and lasts at least the first term. And, three, the President is vulnerable to making a big mistake, the obvious example being the Bay of Pigs or Carter's energy program, which he never made good on."

The idea was to determine through polling what the public thought about specific issues and what their political priorities were. To an extent these are factors which every White House takes into consideration. Jimmy Carter brought on board Jerry Rafshoon, an Atlanta advertising executive, and pollster Pat Caddell to better peddle the President's image to fit the public's desire. Of course, attempts to enhance Jimmy Carter's image never worked for the Carter Administration as well as they have for Reagan's. This was largely because the Carter White House was divided about how far to go, and therefore not as systematic in trying to script Carter's image. Rafshoon argued for fitting the President's appearances before the press to the Administration's purposes. Jody Powell, on the other hand, argued for less control and more access to the President, which is what he believed the press demanded in the aftermath of the Nixon Administration.

The extent to which poll results and politics drove—and continue to drive—Reagan White House policy sometimes seems to have more in common with Procter and Gamble's approach to marketing a new toothpaste than with customary presidential decision-making. Even more striking is the Reaganites openly matter-of-fact approach toward manipulating the presidential image. Previous Administrations have assumed that the hows and whys of presidential image molding, like a woman's beauty secrets, are best kept among friends.

According to Blumenthal, "Gergen had an aide draw up a chart comparing the placement and amount of time being given on the network news to El Salvador and to the economic program. The higher up the story and the longer it runs, the greater its importance, in the White House view, as a public issue. The President's strategists see themselves in constant competition with the network news producers over what appears on the screen and how much it is emphasized. When El Salvador began receiving more time than the economic plan, Gergen showed his colleagues his chart. It was a turning point in the crisis. The White House decided to 'lower the octave.' "

According to White House aide Richard Beal, who previously worked for Reagan pollster Richard Wirthlin, "What was wrong with El Salvador was the packaging of the activity in terms of policy and presentation to the public. It wasn't well staged or sequenced." This concept of the packaging or staging of issues taking precedence over policy and substance is worrisome. It is hardly reassuring to know that the men and women who are running the government are making decisions based chiefly on how they can sell the issue to the public. Leadership means more than eliciting a high rating in the polls or second-guessing the producers of the network newscasts. Similarly, it was troubling that Reagan announced his intention to name a woman to the Supreme Court only after his pollster, Wirthlin, found that the public would approve. Richard Beal put it bluntly: "We knew it was an all-win situation." Although there were other factors in this decision—the original promise was made during the campaign in an effort to bolster Reagan's slumping standing with women voters—the poll results were an important element.

The plan to prolong the President's honeymoon with the press was helped by the Reagan Administration's extraordinary luck in not having to face any major, unscripted events during those first three months. When the first crisis struck—the attempt on the President's life in March 1980—it proved, for all its horror, to be an opportune event for presidential image makers. "It [the assassination attempt] focused uniquely on the President," Richard Beal told the *New York Times*. "It did a lot to endear the President to the people."

Two Presidents: Two Images

Before the shooting, polls showed that Reagan was regarded favorably among respondents by a two-to-one margin. But when Reagan pollsters conducted a survey after the shooting and asked, "As a result of the assassination attempt, have you changed your opinion of Ronald Reagan?" 11 percent said they had. Less than a week after the incident, according to Sidney Blumenthal, Reagan media advisers huddled to discuss strategy on how to invest this new "political capital," to use the words of one White House aide. The result was that Reagan's first major public appearance after his hospitalization was a speech on the economy before a joint session of Congress. Predictably, it received the critical acclaim of the news media, and struck fear into the hearts of many members of Congress planning to vote against the Reagan budget. The courage Reagan displayed in the face of the assassination attempt also did much to endear him to the press. And that sympathy, coupled with their shock over the critical wounding of White House Press Secretary James Brady, made the press more forgiving of the Administration's mistakes in the handling of the story and the daily White House press operations immediately afterwards.

At first glance, Jimmy Carter's and Ronald Reagan's respective effectiveness and choices of official spokesmen contrast sharply with the degree of emphasis these two chief executives placed on their White House media campaigns. Carter, who seemed to underestimate the press, named his closest and most trusted adviser, Jody Powell, as press secretary. Ronald Reagan, who probably overestimates the media's role, reached far outside his inner circle in putting daily press operations in the hands of James Brady and, later, Brady's deputy, Larry Speakes. In fact, the selection of Brady and Speakes, whose access to the inner workings of Reagan and his men was tenuous at best when they began, was another way of ensuring tight control of information from the White House. The choice of Powell, on the other hand, demonstrated Carter's commitment to running an open, accessible Administration.

Jody Powell was both the first and last line of defense for the increasingly besieged Carter Administration. Powell was Carter's greatest asset, and the consensus among White House reporters was that he was very good at his job. Some even said they would have to reach back to Eisenhower's greatly respected spokesman, James Hagerty, to find an equally effective White House press secretary. This is a remarkable tribute, considering that traditionally the press and the President have diametrically opposed views of the role of any press secretary, as former LBJ White House spokesman George Reedy once noted. "Presidents . . . regard the position as a super-duper public relations post whose mission is to build a favorable image of the Chief Executive," Reedy observed. "The press . . . believes that the assignment *should* be to act as a legman digging up stories for White House correspondents." Reedy concluded that the White House press secretary's most important function should be to act as a "point of contact between the President and the press . . . which is vital in a society which operates best when there is a continuing flow of information."

One of the reasons Powell was rated so highly by reporters is that he was exceptionally bright. He came to Washington relatively inexperienced in how the city worked, but he learned quickly, and he never stopped learning. He was a fast study who developed a command of complicated issues and decisions and the ability to hold his own under fire in briefings with reporters. And most of the time he demonstrated good judgment in anticipating the media's reaction to an event or decision. Some of the credit for the success of the 1978 Camp David summit, for example, belongs to Powell. While a pack of several hundred restless reporters awaited the outcome of

Carter's attempt to hammer out a peace plan for the Middle East with Israeli Prime Minister Menachem Begin and Egyptian President Anwar Sadat, Powell managed to keep reporters' expectations from soaring. The agreement that was reached, while far from perfect, was interpreted at the time as a great victory for Jimmy Carter.

But, as with Carter, there was a darker side to Powell's personality. He could be devious, deceptive, and even personally biting at times with reporters. For example. I remember one angry crack he made to me when I pressed him for an answer to a question. The incident occurred just two days after Carter fired Andrew Young as ambassador to the United Nations for contradicting the Administration's policy by privately meeting with officials of the Palestine Liberation Organization. At the time, we were all traveling with the President, who was making a week's cruise down the Mississippi River aboard the *Delta Queen*. During one of the riverside stops, reporters gathered around Powell in a boathouse, peppering him with questions about the bitter controversy over Young's firing. I threw one in and persisted, although I could sense that Powell was growing testier by the minute. "Well, Judy," he shot back, "just because you didn't have time to fix your hair this morning doesn't mean you have to take it out on me."

This acerbic side of Powell created some problems in his handling of the press. Then too, he tended to take criticism of the Administration personally, leading him to overreact at times. When White House aide Hamilton Jordan was accused in the *Washington Post* of spitting a drink down a woman's dress in a Washington bar, Powell commissioned a thirty-three-page rebuttal that made the incident an even bigger story.

These faults aside, Powell did generally demonstrate considerable intelligence and judgment. His greatest strength as a White House spokesman, however, was his closeness to the

President. He had worked on Jimmy Carter's first campaign for governor in 1966, and over the years an almost father-son relationship had developed. When Powell walked into the White House briefing room, you could normally tell by his mood what the President's mood was that day. He had access to virtually every decision that was made in the White House. When Powell spoke from the briefing room podium, reporters knew either that what he said was what was going on or that it was as much as Powell wanted you to know.

With Ronald Reagan, on the other hand, there was no White House press spokesman who had been close to him from the very beginning. Lyn Nofziger, who was very close to Reagan while he was governor of California, came as close as anyone to playing the role of trusted media adviser during the campaign. But after the election he was named assistant to the President for political affairs, and after a year in that job, left the White House altogether. Lou Cannon, who knows Reagan better than I, says the newly elected President considered himself his own best media adviser, and believed there was no necessity for a press secretary with a long-standing relationship with him.

The man chosen as White House press secretary, James Brady, had worked in the short-lived presidential campaign of Texas' John Connally before enlisting in the Reagan camp, where he gradually won the respect of several on the staff. Brady possessed a wonderful sense of humor, and enjoyed poking fun with reporters as well as at them. After Reagan suggested during the campaign that trees help cause air pollution, it was Brady who coined the phrase "killer trees."

Probably because of such irreverence, Brady was slow to gain the Reaganites' trust. It was well into the transition period between Reagan's election and inauguration before the President-elect's senior advisers picked Brady to be the White House press secretary. There had been suspicion that Brady had been the source of some leaks during the campaign. There was also talk that he had not won Nancy Reagan's support. Rumor had it that she didn't think Brady was handsome enough to be her husband's press secretary, and Reagan joked about that when he announced Brady's appointment. He was just beginning to feel comfortable in the job when John Hinckley shot him. Brady's tragic, abrupt departure from the White House threw a wrench into the well-oiled Reagan media machine. The confusion that resulted in Brady's absence from the White House briefing room on the day of the assassination attempt was just the beginning.

Instead of establishing a clear line of communication between the President and the press, the Administration divided the job of press relations between Brady's deputy, Larry Speakes, and David Gergen, author of "The First 100 Days" plan, who, with the title Assistant to the President for Communications, technically outranked Speakes. For almost a full year, they shared daily briefing chores: Speakes on Mondays, Wednesdays, and Fridays; and Gergen on Tuesdays and Thursdays. For reporters, the initial confusion over who was *really* in control of the White House press operation overall as well as whom to turn to for information from day to day was like a game of media musical chairs. Since then we have learned to live with two press secretaries and to recognize the strengths and weaknesses of each.

Like Brady, Larry Speakes had to start from scratch in winning the trust of Reagan insiders. A former public relations man, Speakes was initially labeled a lightweight by some White House aides and reporters. But his folksy, familiar manner is deceptive. Behind the toothy smile and the down-home speech of his native Mississippi is a shrewd political infighter. The proof of this is that Speakes rebounded from the early criticism in less than a year to win the praise and confidence of the Reagan triumvirate—Meese, Deaver, and Baker.

"This is Judy Woodruff at the White House"

No doubt as the mood in the White House press room grew more critical of the Administration, Reagan's advisers recognized that Speakes's unflappability in the face of antagonistic questioning by reporters is a valuable asset. While Speakes delivers the Administration's party line, he does it with grace under pressure and a thick skin. He normally doesn't take personally the hostilities that sometimes emerge during briefings. Reporters have come to expect from him quick-to-the-point answers—even when the Administration wants only a minimum of information released. Still, Speakes does not enjoy unlimited access to the President and his inner policy circle. And while Gergen, who gave up regular briefings in early 1982, sometimes had more access, he often wasn't as nimble as Speakes in ducking controversies. Instead, he earnestly tried to answer nearly all questions.

Both Speakes and Gergen are Southerners. But, as Howell Raines noted in a late 1981 *New York Times* profile of the two men, Gergen "grew up in North Carolina but he has lost the ability to act like a Southerner, having been to Yale." Raines added, "Mr. Speakes preserved this ability by attending the University of Mississippi. More than a decade after leaving the Delta, he clings to the down-home locution of placing honorifics in front of given names, as in Miss Betsy or Mister Dave." (Raines, in a wonderful description of the tall, gangling Gergen, wrote that the communications chief's ambling manner and six-foot-five-inch frame create the impression that he was kidnapped as a child and raised by giraffes.)

As competitors of sorts, Speakes and Gergen are less than crazy about each other, but they do share one common bond: neither has as much access to the President as Jody Powell enjoyed. But as long as the goal is control, rather than information, this probably serves President Reagan's purposes well. This certainly was the case with the Reagan Administration's handling of news conferences. Whereas during the Carter

Administration, and for years prior to it, reporters were recognized by jumping up out of their seats and shouting, "Mr. President," the Reagan team changed the rules. The Reagan staff decreed that after the President called on the senior wire-service reporters, which was customary, all other reporters would be permitted only to raise their hands. We were told to remain in our seats and keep quiet. That rule has remained in effect throughout the Reagan presidency.

But another scheme, devised for Reagan's second news conference on March sixth, fortunately did not survive. It was nicknamed the jellybean lottery. At the suggestion of his media advisers, the President drew names of reporters on slips of paper from a huge jelly bean urn, in the order they would be permitted to ask questions. Since there was no suspense about who might be called on, and since many reporters didn't show up because they had not made the "cut," the news conference lost a great deal of spontaneity. After the assassination attempt that spring, there were no more news conferences until June 1981, and by then we were back to raising our hands and wearing loud colors to try to attract Mr. Reagan's attention.

My preparation for news conferences has been similar for both Presidents. I find it useful to reread clippings I've collected since the last news conference, which means, during the Reagan Administration, a rather large file, since his conferences have been held anywhere from one to three months apart. It is also helpful to call a number of people around Washington for their views and suggested questions. I may not always take their advice, but I gain a sense of how the President is being perceived by his allies and his adversaries. For example, to prepare for one Reagan news conference in March 1982, I called both a prominent Democratic congressman and a senior staff assistant to a leading Republican senator, because both had been involved in recent budget negotiations, albeit from different perspectives.

My colleague Lee Lescaze, who formerly covered the White

House for the *Washington Post,* explained why news conferences should favor the President: "As most presidents have known from the beginning, or learned very quickly, you don't have to answer the tough questions. You can skate around them. You can take one aspect of a question and talk about something you like that's vaguely related. At the same time you can look Presidential. You can look calm and collected in the face of a barrage of questions. Followups, although they exist, aren't really troublesome because you don't get badgered. No one's going to be rude to the President," Lescaze said in a magazine interview this year.

This was true for Jimmy Carter. His media adviser Greg Schneiders says Carter was an ideal "news conference" president, because he was such a quick study and had such an impressive command of facts that reporters found it difficult to challenge him. In fact, he was so well programmed that it was difficult to elicit spontaneous, newsworthy quotes from him. A rare exception I played a major role in was his answer to a question I asked in 1977 about federal funding for abortions. After he responded to my first question by saying he didn't think this was the proper role for government, I asked if he thought it was fair that women who could afford to have abortions may have them, while women who cannot must go ahead and have babies they don't want. His answer was one of his few memorable lines. "Well, as you know, Judy," he said, "there are many things in life that are unfair." Another news conference performance that hurt more than it helped occurred in the summer of 1980, when a reporter forced him to back down from an assertion that it was Ronald Reagan, and not his own Secretary of Health and Human Services, Patricia Harris, who had first brought up the subject of racism in that year's campaign. Still, Carter's discipline and mastery of detail stood him in good stead, even during such testy periods of his presidency as the summer of 1980, when his brother Billy was drawing unfavorable attention to the President because of his relations with the Libyan regime of Colonel Khaddafy. In one hour-long evening news conference, televised live on all three networks, Carter managed to tackle the "Billy" issue and, in so doing, defuse some of the criticism that was hurting him as he prepared for the Democratic nominating convention.

For Ronald Reagan, on the other hand, news conferences during his first year in office turned into an ordeal involving marathon briefing sessions by his advisers. They frequently stood off to the side during the news conference holding their breath, waiting to see if the President would make some misstatement, or recall an anecdote about a welfare queen which could not be verified. Because Reagan did not bring the self-discipline to news conferences that his predecessor did, his aides began, early in 1982, to institute "issues luncheons" every Monday to bring the President up-to-date on the status of major issues of the day. Reagan's problems with little facts and stories seemed to reach a peak in late 1981, when Deputy Press Secretary Larry Speakes scurried around the press room immediately after a news conference, telling reporters that the President had not meant to close the door on a tax increase, even though Mr. Reagan had said, "I have no plans for increasing taxes in any way." The next month, Reagan told columnist Mary McGrory that the reason he didn't give more money to charity was that he tithed. White House aides later acknowledged that the President hadn't meant to suggest that he actually gave one-tenth of his income to charity every year. At the same news conference, he gave some unemployment statistics that turned out to be incorrect, and the White House explained that they had actually been "averages" of figures used over a longer period of time—a method economics reporters were not familiar with.

The "gaffe" problem grew to such proportions that it became an issue of considerable concern to the White House staff. So much so, that when the President completed a news conference in March 1982 without making any obvious "misstatements," Larry Speakes pranced about the press room afterwards with a huge smile on his face. How long that euphoria would last no one could say, however. As former Reagan campaign manager John Sears points out, Reagan normally is very good about catching his own mistakes and defusing them before they cause a problem. But under the intense pressure of the presidency, and with the enormous amount of information a President is expected to absorb, it's not clear that Reagan will always feel the incentive to do his homework, week in and week out. As for Reagan's penchant for anecdotes, Sears says the staff will always run the risk of being caught off guard. "His problem is he's got all these records in his head," says Sears, "and he'll grab for one of them on the shelf and pull out the record, and play it in full." Sears continues, "those records were formed many years ago. They're oldies but goodies, and nobody's been able to get into his record library and change it."

All Presidents must face up to the fact that the honeymoon with the press eventually ends. But Reagan's prolonged romance with the news media seemed to make the growing criticism of him and his policies in the early spring of 1982 fall on him like a ton of bricks. Everywhere he looked in the print press and on television, Reagan seemed to be under attack. His policy in El Salvador, seemingly based on a resurrection of the "domino theory," was being decried as drawing the country dangerously close to another Vietnam complete with evening TV news reports of gunfire from the guerilla battlefields. Reaganomics, the most ambitious economic recovery plan undertaken by a President since Franklin D. Roosevelt's New Deal, had yet to prove it was the cure-all Reagan had promised. Another promise, to balance the budget by 1984, was looking more and more like a pipe dream. What's more, cracks began to show in his credibility as he tried to retreat from the balanced budget pledge by saying it was never a promise, only a goal. Television footage of Reagan broadcast during an NBC White Paper on his presidency in December 1981 glaringly proved otherwise. There for several million viewers to see was a clip of candidate Reagan saying, "The fact is this [economic] program will give us a balanced budget by 1983; possibly by 1982."

Unemployment was the highest since the Great Depression. But Reagan's budgetmeisters planned to slash even deeper into social welfare programs for the needy. Meanwhile, his wife, Nancy, was still recovering from criticism for her move to restock the White House china cupboard. More and more, Ronald Reagan began to look like a President who was callously indifferent to the poor. "Reagan's America: And The Poor Get Poorer," read a *Newsweek* magazine cover which featured a photo of a poor child in a dirty dress. It was the sort of image that drives White House image makers to commit hari-kari.

Even newspaper comics pages derided the President for his tendency to get his facts twisted during press conferences. With stinging humor, "Doonesbury" featured a strip of a Reagan news conference on the budget with a Sam Donaldson-like character excitedly telling the President, "Mr. President, if you make another mistake, you're going to break your all-time record for mistakes."

In a March 1982 interview with the Daily *Oklahoman,* Reagan's frustration boiled over and he fired back what was for him an unusual but not unprecedented attack on the press. (He had lashed out similarly at times in California.) He charged the networks with delaying his economic recovery with their "constant downbeat stories." "Is it news," he asked, "that some fellow out in South Succotash someplace has just been laid off, that he should be interviewed nationwide, or someone's complaint that the budget cuts are going to hurt their present program?"

At the time, NBC's John Chancellor responded this way: "Pictures of any problem that a society has, and this society has a serious economic problem . . . are not going to create an optimistic attitude. There's nothing upbeat about that. But that effect is probably not as important as the fundamental things troubling the economy. It's impossible to run a society like ours without showing pictures like that. According to the polls, unemployment and inflation are right at the top of everyone's list of concerns, so journalism has a responsibility to cover them."

But a few days after this outburst Reagan retreated. "I hope I didn't touch a nerve with any of the press a few days ago," he said in a digression from a speech, "because I think that most of the time the overwhelming majority of them are doing a fine job, and as a former reporter, columnist, and commentator myself, I know just how tough it can be."

Behind this presidential fence mending, I suspect, lay some very shrewd reasoning. While there is no doubt that the President genuinely believed he was being treated unfairly by the press, he also realized that to unleash his anger publicly would only hurt him and, as happened with Jimmy Carter, could easily escalate a conflict into open warfare. That is the last thing any President needs, particularly one who enjoys Reagan's popularity with reporters.

What had been even more astounding, though, was the President's suggestion in a *TV Guide* interview at about the same time that the press should "trust us [the government] and put themselves in our hands and say, 'I have a story,' if it involves a national security or other sensitive issue." The President added that the government could then explain "what we're trying to accomplish," and presumably the press would then withhold the story. Instead, he lamented, "they just go with the story—and we read it."

Mr. Reagan's feelings are understandable. As former State Department spokesman Hodding Carter reminded us in a column he wrote for the *Wall Street Journal* in early 1982, "Presidents have always made other press critics sound like pantywaists. The more Jefferson came to experience what his First Amendment had produced, the less he liked it. And Harry Truman probably spoke for all his fellow presidents when he wrote, 'I really look with commiseration over the great body of my fellow citizens who, reading newspapers, live and die in the belief that they have known something of what has been passing in their time.' " But the idea of trusting the government to decide what stories should or shouldn't be published or broadcast is so ludicrous that even conservative allies of Mr. Reagan in the press took issue with the President's plea. While the aim of politicians, including Mr. Reagan, is more often than not to present a case in its most favorable light, that is not always synonymous with its most accurate light. It's true that there may be something of a "Vietnam syndrome" among reporters in the 1970s and '80s. It's true that the press is sometimes too cynical. But there is a reason for that syndrome: the government lied to the people and the press during the Vietnam ordeal. As for the overall coverage of El Salvador, the media are not the only ones that see cracks in the Reagan policies (and I think the coverage here has been much more balanced than the President realizes), but even Administration insiders have been critical. It's no secret that Defense Secretary Caspar Weinberger is among them.

It's easy to understand why the President is displeased with some of the recent economic coverage. As of the spring of 1982 his policies had yet to create the successes he predicted, and public disillusionment was on the rise. Unemployment is climbing to its highest levels since 1941, which means that there are a lot of fellows being laid off out there in "South Succotash" and elsewhere. It certainly would be irresponsible not to put some of them on the air when discussing the economy. Indeed, during the 1980 campaign, when there were more than two million *fewer* unemployed persons than in early 1982, Ronald Reagan was positively eloquent in describing and publicizing, as often as possible, their plight. What has changed is not television news coverage but Reagan's perspective and political interests.

For all their differences, the one element clearly common to both the Carter and Reagan presidencies, and to every other modern-day Administration as well, is this adversarial relationship with the press: A relationship whereby the press "checks" the actions of the presidency, to assure they serve the public's best interests. Without a press, government officials could conduct their affairs in any manner they pleased. For any reporter, the trick in successfully covering Jimmy Carter or Ronald Reagan is to walk that thin line of maintaining skepticism without lapsing into cynicism; of cultivating and creating mutual trust with informative sources without becoming so involved that detachment is impossible; and of understanding and appreciating the President's strengths and weaknesses without personalizing either. In the end, a quasi-adversarial relationship is inevitable and probably even healthy. From our viewpoint it would be disastrous to, as President Reagan suggested in his *TV Guide* interview, put ourselves in the hands of the administration, cede to government the power to determine whether certain news stories should run. We would become political appendages. In exercising our own judgment we occasionally abuse our freedom, but then the founding fathers never suggested that freedom of the press was applicable only to the "responsible" press. As uncomfortable as those occasional abuses make us at times, they are far preferable to any government dictation of news coverage. Can you imagine Richard Nixon directing coverage of Watergate?

Two Presidents: Two Images

I suspect that this adversarial relationship is healthy for politicians, too. In 1961, for example, the *New York Times* had information that the Kennedy Administration was planning to launch an invasion of Cuba. The newspaper, on patriotic grounds, decided not to publish the story. The invasion took place, and the result was the Bay of Pigs disaster. President Kennedy later confided that he wished the *Times* had been a bit more "irresponsible" in that instance.

Yet few politicians will ever appreciate this. "Presidents are politicians and politicians always see the press as an arena for warfare," George Reedy wrote last year in the *Boston University Communications Review.* "The concept that a newspaper or a television news presentation exists to foster the political dialogue in a free society is incomprehensible to the political mind. In a lifetime of observing politicians—from the ward level in Chicago when I was a child, to the White House when I was fully mature—one aspect of their personalities has been consistent. It is that all of them believed that stories were written to advance or retard a cause—not because something had happened. This factor is at the root of the running warfare that has characterized the relations between the press and the Presidency since the days of George Washington. The basic problem is that politicians and journalists literally see different worlds. The politician classifies people in terms of friend or foe, and sees no reason to exempt the journalist from such classification. The journalist classifies people in terms of those 'who tell it straight,' and those 'who tell it crooked,' and the journalist cannot accept the reasoning of the partisan that whatever advances a 'noble' cause is the 'straight way' of telling the story."

Reedy concludes: "These differing viewpoints promote an adversary relationship which intensifies in proportion to the degree of honesty held by the participants. The theme song of the White House press room should be a parody of Kipling's

'East is East and West is West and never the twain shall meet.' "

Having covered two Presidents, I agree with Reedy's analysis. As different in philosophy as were Jimmy Carter and Ronald Reagan, they both experienced their share of what they would term "hostile" press coverage. It is unfortunate that they viewed it as such, but critical coverage is inevitable. And the very fact that every modern President, regardless of his political philosophy, has been through the same sort of skeptical treatment belies the notion that the press is too liberal, or ideological in approach. What does concern me, however, is that some reporters come to believe their mission is to tear down the President: to assume he's done wrong before the facts are in, and to interpret every decision in a cynical light. The ultimate result may be the tearing down of the institution of the presidency.

Multimedia Marriage

There are probably as many preconceived ideas about what makes a successful marriage as there are divorced couples. If we've learned anything from the social upheavals of the last two decades, it is that preconceived notions no longer fit the patterns of our lives and the various roles we play. Perhaps they never really did. That is why I find the dark pictures painted of two-career marriages are frequently short-sighted. Yes, there are pressures involved in combining career and marriage. But there are also some very decided advantages. And does anyone think that single-career marriages are without pressures?

For those who believe that a smoothly run house, quiet evenings together, and never bringing your work home with you make for a happy marriage, Al's and my life together may seem like a high-wire act teetering dangerously close to disaster. We have closets in our house that remind me of the black hole of Calcutta. But I think that couples whose lives more closely resemble ours will recognize, as we do, that despite the conflicting schedules and separate travel, two careers can be very enriching to a marriage. Our time apart makes our time together that much more precious. Taking each other for granted is a luxury we don't have.

Still, it's a delicate balancing act. Sharing the same profession makes it easier because we each know the peculiar demands of the news business all too well. Al doesn't get upset when I miss dinner to work late on a story any more than I do when he's late. And I don't feel guilty about missing dinner any more than he does.

But even more important than sharing the same profession, we share the same level of dedication to our careers. We also both derive a great deal of personal satisfaction from those careers, which can't help but spill over into our marriage. I believe that if you feel good about your work—whether it's homemaking or news reporting—then you feel good about yourself, and that can only enhance your relationship with your spouse. But it cuts the other way, too. There is nothing like the security of loving and being loved to give you a healthier perspective on yourself, your work.

For us, all this adds up to a marriage that works. What is more, we wouldn't have it any other way. I could no more imagine myself as a traditional homemaking wife than Al could imagine himself as a breadwinning nine-to-five husband. It helps that we knew this about ourselves and each other going into our marriage.

I always knew that I wanted a lifelong career, as well as a husband and family. Although my mother is a full-time homemaker, she always encouraged the idea of careers for me and my sister, Anita, who is a teacher. If there is one bit of advice she gave me that stands out in my mind, it is: "diapers and dishes can wait." Mother worked before and during the first years of her marriage, and probably would have continued to work except for the continuous shuffling of military life.

Managing a career and a marriage, I assumed, would all magically work out. But by the time I celebrated my thirtieth birthday, still single, my mother was no longer repeating those homespun words of wisdom to me and I was beginning to lose faith in magic. Then, three months after I arrived in Washington, I was seated at a table next to Al Hunt in "Clyde's," a popular Georgetown cafe. I was there for a shop-talk dinner with Bob Jamieson, who was then also covering the White House for NBC, and Al was dining with Edie Wilkie, a good friend.

Our first encounter had been on the Carter campaign, as we stood in adjacent phone booths in a Steubenville, Ohio, shopping center calling our news desks. Before he had a chance to introduce himself, the waiting press bus revved up its engine to warn straggling reporters that it was time to depart, and I tore off. We met a few weeks later in Plains, Georgia, while I was playing second base and he was fielding in one of the ritual softball games between the Carter campaign staff and the press. He claims he would have asked me out that night but he had a date with a stewardess in Atlanta. She must have been *some* stewardess, because Atlanta is more than a three-hour drive from Plains.

We both left the Carter campaign shortly afterwards. I returned to Atlanta to cover other stories for NBC, and Al went off to cover other candidates for the *Wall Street Journal*. The softball game was the last time I had seen him until that night in Georgetown. Since I was new to Washington and acquainted with very few people in town, his familiar shock of prematurely gray hair was a welcome sight.

"Well, how are you getting along?" he asked.

"Miserably," I replied. "I've been living out of a suitcase in the Watergate Hotel for the past six weeks and I haven't even had time to unpack, much less to look for an apartment. I'm homesick."

Within four months of that meeting at "Clyde's," we were, as they say in the Washington gossip columns, "an item," and I was no longer homesick. Our courtship was squeezed in between conflicting schedules, work-related cocktail parties and receptions and out-of-town assignments, which often meant that I was on the road when he was home and vice versa. It probably sounds amazing that we ever came to know each other well enough to marry. But looking back, I think the crazy-quilt nature of our schedules may have helped bring us together.

We found out how much we missed and trusted each other when we were apart. And we found out how much we depended on each other when we were together. When I was discouraged or frustrated about work, I could pour my heart out to Al and know that he really understood and that his advice was based on the perspective that comes with experience. His emotional support was tremendously helpful to me as I struggled to get my professional bearings in a new job and a new town. I was able to give him support in other ways. Washington and Washington journalism are governed by a what-have-you-done-for-me-lately mentality, and after a while it can wear you down. I think I came along at a time in Al's life when he really needed to feel that there was somebody in his corner whether he had the lead story on the front page that day or last month, somebody who liked him and loved him for what he was, not what he did.

When we decided in the fall of 1979 to set a wedding date, we had to work it into the approaching 1980 presidential campaign calendar. Tentatively, we agreed on January 5— well before the political campaigns would begin full-swing but late enough to avoid stiffer taxes. Early in November I suggested to Al that we should begin making arrangements for the wedding.

"Gosh, honey," he said, sheepishly, "I've got to be in the *Des Moines Register* debate." Al never did get his chance to question the two candidates because the event never took place. Jimmy Carter backed out of that debate with his major rival, Ted Kennedy, citing the Iranian hostages as an excuse. By then, we had already settled on April 5, a day which coincided with the longest break between presidential primaries.

Although our wedding had all the trappings of tradition— the ceremony was held in St. Alban's Episcopal Church, the bride wore white lace, the groom a gray morning suit—we knew from our courtship that our marriage would be anything but old-fashioned. My decision to retain my maiden name so as not to confuse people who knew me professionally was perhaps the most apparent indication of that. In the years since my wedding, however, having a different last name from my husband has sometimes produced more confusion than it has dispelled. Certainly, there have been some raised eyebrows along the way.

One of the most amusing misunderstandings occurred in Oxfordshire, England, where we were attending a political seminar with, among others, my NBC colleague Roger Mudd. The seminar was held at a magnificent English countryside estate, Ditchley, where Al and I shared a room attended by a very proper English butler named Travis. Each morning, Travis would serve us breakfast in bed, always careful to greet me as "Miss Woodruff" and Al as "Mr. Hunt." Still, we became friendly enough with him that on the day before we departed Al mentioned that we were expecting a baby. Travis seemed quite taken aback, until Al explained that we were married.

"You know, sir," the visibly relieved butler said, "I couldn't figure you and Miss Woodruff out. I looked at your addresses when you arrived (we had given our office addresses) and noticed that Miss Woodruff and Mr. Mudd stayed together back in the States. But over here, poor old Mr. Mudd is up alone in Room 25, while Miss Woodruff is with you in Room 10."

While it may seem like a long shot that two people in the same profession would wind up married to each other, multimedia marriages are uncommonly common in Washington.

155

The most famous media couple, of course, is Ben Bradlee, executive editor of the *Washington Post* and his wife Sally Quinn, the paper's star feature writer. The *Post*'s Justice Department reporter, Mary Thornton, is married to Curtis Wilkie, White House correspondent for the *Boston Globe*. White House correspondent Michael Putzel and his wife, Anne Blackman, a feature writer, both report for Associated Press. And Steve Roberts of the *New York Times* and his wife, Cokie, of National Public Radio, share the same beat—Congress.

Husbands and wives sharing the same profession, however, is not unique to journalism. Sociologist Caroline Bird, author of *The Two Paycheck Marriage,* points out that a surprising number of couples share careers in such fields as fashion, entertainment, publishing, research, and education. She reported: "Many of the stablest two-career marriages are between people in the same occupation or on the same professional network." What it boils down to, I think, is simply that common interests attract, and the more absorbing the common interest, the stronger the attraction. That doesn't necessarily make for the best relationship, although in our field I think it's an advantage. Bird notes that the fields with a predominance of married couples tend to be those that depend on the exchange of information and that "a spouse in the business can double the flow of that information."

I don't know what entertainers or sociologists talk about, but I do know that journalists' conversations are often dominated by the news. It might strike some people as bizarre, but often Al's or my first words to each other over our morning coffee may be such intimacies as, "Did you see the White House piece in the *Times*?" Or, "Haig was really tough on the 'Today' show." I also doubt that many people plan their Sundays around watching politicians and government officials on TV interview shows.

But apart from sharing a common interest, I think there are aspects peculiar to the news business that may also explain why two by-line bedrooms are so prevalent and why journalists make good marriage partners.

First of all, only a saint or another journalist could tolerate a reporter's work schedule. I certainly dated my share of men who simply couldn't understand it when my work interfered with their plans for dinner or sailing or vacations. To be sure, they worked hard in their jobs, too. But they also were able to draw lines between their careers and their personal lives—something journalists just cannot do.

During the first seven months of our marriage, Al was on the campaign trail eighty percent of the time. And after staying in Washington for two months while Carter campaigned from the Rose Garden, I began to travel almost as much. At times during the campaign we had to make dates to see each other. After one separation, I was assigned to follow Rosalyn Carter to Philadelphia, where she was making a speech, at the same time that Al was there doing a story on the upcoming Pennsylvania primary. Our itineraries made it sensible to stay in different hotels, but we seized our chance to see each other by arranging a rendezvous for dinner. Unfortunately, I ended up working so late that night that it never came off. Still, as much as I wanted to see Al and he wanted to see me, we both knew that in this case work had to come first. But how many nonreporter husbands or wives would feel that way? By the same token, if I were a homemaker, I'm not sure I would have put up with Al's campaigning. I also doubt that I would have seen any more of Al during those first seven months as a news-widowed bride.

Another side of the news business that I suspect multimedia couples may find it easier to adjust to is the curious hold it has on the people involved. The term *news business* is probably a misnomer—it's actually more of an addiction. Partly because of ego, partly professional pride, partly the competitive nature of reporting, when an important news event occurs I want to be the one NBC wakes in the middle of the night to cover it. Al feels the same way about his paper. That drive has got to be difficult for nonjournalists to understand, to say nothing of the extraordinary patience that the inevitable missed dinners, theater performances, and anniversary celebrations require.

I've even been late to a few of my own dinner parties because of late-breaking stories. Fortunately, my friends understand the situation. One evening while Al and I were still dating I was so caught up in nailing down a story on nuclear proliferation for the "Today" show that I never made it home in time to prepare dinner for our guests. Mary McGrory, the well-known Washington columnist, charged into the kitchen, where Al was desperately scouring the refrigerator for more cheese and crackers to placate his starving guests, and began preparing dinner for everyone.

"Judy may be a wonderful girl, Al, and I hope the two of you are terribly happy," Mary joked, "but I'm not going to go the whole night without eating."

I've since learned to solve the problem of disrupted dinner parties by preparing simple dishes well in advance, or by ordering dinner from one of the many take-out catering services in Washington, so that Al can take over if necessary and the show can go on without me. What we lack in gourmet meals, I feel, we make up in fun and interesting people and conversation. Al agrees. But if he were a corporate executive or diplomat whose career advancement hinged on his wife's ability to reign as the perfect hostess, frankly I don't know how we would do it.

Certainly there are other businesses and professions that entail equally long hours and equally arduous schedules. My brother-in-law, Bill Hunt, is a highly dedicated family physician in Quarryville, Pennsylvania, who averages more than eighty hours a week caring for his patients. But few other vocations are as persistently unpredictable or unsettling emotionally as journalism. There is a wonderful high in breaking an important story or doing an especially insightful piece. But the emotional volatility of the job also has its down side. Getting beaten on a major story, not getting on the air or in the newspaper for a while, or flailing in frustration over an elusive story can be downright depressing. These highs and lows can, and often do, alternate from day to day.

Working in the same business does not necessarily make it any easier for one partner to cope with the emotional baggage the other brings home from the office at night. No job is going to help you to know how to comfort, reassure, or cheer up your spouse. You learn that from each other. We've had our share of evenings when the bad day only one of us experienced cast a pall over the atmosphere for both of us. But experiencing the same emotional pressures has to make you better equipped to accept those mood swings in yourself and in your partner, if only because you know that tomorrow you may be the one kicking the dog and snapping at your spouse. There's a natural tendency when you're down about work to feel even worse because you've blown off steam at home. Knowing that Al relies on me for understanding when he needs it is as important as having his understanding when I need it. I think it strengthens our marriage. We don't have to put on happy faces for each other. Nor do we feel guilty if the pressures of work sometimes make our tempers flare at home.

Many professions have their ups and downs, but I think the emotional swings are more dramatic in our highly visible vocation. An analyst once called Washington reporters "shy egomaniacs," and it's nice to have someone around who understands those crazy-quilt feelings.

It surprises me how often I'm asked about the competitive

pressures, bruised egos, and conflicts of being married to someone in the same profession. I can honestly say that in the five years we've been together—two of those as husband and wife—I've never felt that Al and I competed against each other on either a personal or a professional level. For me, trying to explain why we don't feel competition between ourselves is rather like trying to answer the old question, "Do you still beat your wife?" But I think the idea that competition goes hand-in-hand with sharing the same profession isn't at all applicable in our case. Al and I not only love each other a lot, but we also respect each other a great deal. I take a lot of personal pride and joy in his accomplishments. We each want the other to succeed and be as happy professionally as we are together personally.

Occasionally, there are situations when possible conflicts of interest arise, especially for multimedia couples whose jobs revolve around the exchange of information. Drawing the line between shop talk and pillow talk, however, is really just a matter of common sense and mutual trust and respect. There have been times when we had to refrain from discussing stories we both were pursuing. But it's not as though we had any big discussion about it, or felt compelled to establish any ground rules. In those situations, we don't even have to say, "I can't talk to you about that," because neither of us expects or would ask the other to talk about it.

During the first round of the Reagan budget cuts, Al was working on an inside look at how the Administration put together the budget package, who won and who lost politically, and the role played by budget director David Stockman. In order to do the story, Al met regularly with Stockman for weeks in advance, with the understanding that none of the information that Stockman revealed would appear until after the budget package was announced. While Al was meeting regularly with Stockman, I was scrambling at the White House trying to turn up any news I could regarding where cuts would be made. My repeated calls to the budget director were unavailing.

Actually, I found out about the Stockman meetings inadvertently. Since we don't play games with one another when it comes to our professional responsibilities, Al readily admitted he was working on the story, but we both knew that was as far as we could go. There were still times that I voiced frustrations over the difficulty I was having fleshing out some of the budget cut details, but Al remained poker-faced throughout my complaints. We never doubted for a moment that the situation would have been identical if the shoe had been on the other foot.

As competitive as we in the news business are, even sometimes with our co-workers, we are still bound by a degree of loyalty to our news organizations that is matched by few professionals and their employers. When I run across a piece of news involving say, Congress, I want NBC to have the story. Although it may also be something in which Al would be interested, I'd automatically give it to an NBC reporter first—in this case John Dancy or Bob Kur, our congressional correspondents. And I know that Al passes along bits of information first to the *Journal*'s White House reporter, Rich Jaroslovsky.

All this may sound a little too "proper." It isn't. Of course we trade gossip and information; we just make a distinction between that kind of information and information one of us or one of our colleagues can confirm and use in a news story. I don't think that is any different from a psychiatrist, or lawyer, or doctor refraining from discussing clients with a spouse. Still, the times when we feel we must refrain from discussing particular stories are greatly outweighed by the help we are able to provide each other. This apparently is true of most couples who share the same profession, according to Caroline

Bird. "Married competitors have more to gain by exchanging information than they have to lose by divulging an occasional 'secret,' " she notes. "As in the nineteenth-century marriages of property, a mutual economic interest stabilizes these unions."

If Al is working on a long, relatively "timeless" feature story, he often shows it to me to get a reaction. Similarly, if I am trying to develop a more comprehensive piece, I will often bounce it off him. I try to read the *Journal* every day and he tries to catch the "NBC Nightly News" each evening, although the timing of the Senate's sessions and of campaign schedules sometimes are not very accommodating. I frequently ask his opinion of my broadcasts, although I have come to expect more praise than I think I deserve. And whenever possible, I watch him on PBS's "Washington Week In Review" and try to critique his performances objectively. Occasionally, I remind him to sit up straighter and not talk so much like an insider that he loses his audience.

We also often serve as sounding boards for each other's views. We compare notes on the news figures we cover—what motivates them, are they on the level, how much of a factor are they in an issue or decision—and we share opinions on events and predictions of their outcomes. I'm sure this helps shape our professional interpretations and analyses.

Sometimes we disagree. Al's appraisal of Jimmy Carter's presidency tended to be more critical than mine, and we had one or two pretty heated debates over the dinner table.

One of the nicest advantages of being married to someone in the same profession is that we are able to travel together on the same professional circuit, whether it's work-related social functions or occasional reporting assignments on the road. Through each other we have made contacts in our work that we might not have made separately. I've met many senators, congressmen, and congressional staffers due to Al's wide-ranging sources on Capitol Hill. Likewise, during the Carter years, I helped Al with some of the Georgians.

We probably also receive invitations as a couple that we might not receive individually. Every Administration occasionally invites the correspondents who cover the President to White House social functions. Al likes to joke that in twelve years in Washington he never was asked to a state dinner until he married me.

On the other hand, the first time I met Ronald Reagan was because of Al's invitation to a Reagan press party shortly before the election campaign. Because Al had covered the Reagan campaign, he was the one invited to the barbecue the Republican nominee hosted at the estate in Middleburg, Virginia, where he resided during the last half of 1980. I was keenly aware that some of the Reagan loyalists at the party regarded me as something of a political mole, since I was covering the enemy camp. But Al just nudged me toward an empty chair next to Reagan, who was regaling a cluster of guests with a story about his father-in-law—and, some say, political mentor—Dr. Loyal Davis. Some years ago, Reagan told his listeners, Davis was honored by a group of Russians after he performed life-saving surgery on a Soviet military officer. After the dinner, several people noticed that some of the silver flatware was missing, but no one spoke up. Finally, Davis rose to complain about the disappearance. It wasn't long, according to Reagan, before the Soviet officials began emptying their pockets of the silverware.

"That just goes to show you that you can't trust the Commies," declared the Republican nominee for President. "They'll do anything."

Because we have made many of the same contacts in social situations, we sometimes unwittingly turn to the same sources on stories. There have been times when I've called a source on a story and the source said, "Hey, I just got a call from Al," or the other way around. Sometimes a source will assume that telling Al is as good as telling me, and I always explain that that's not the way it works. Other times I can pretty well guess who that unidentified source in one of Al's stories is, and I'm sure he can do the same with me. When we both covered Ronald Reagan on vacation in August, 1981, a high Administration official phoned Al at our rented home several times over several days, and I answered, recognizing the voice. Invariably, the day after the "Mystery Caller" phoned, Al would make the paper with bits of news on the continuing budget story, which I was also covering. But knowing who that source was did me little good. I'd been trying him for days before that without any luck.

Combining two careers with marriage often becomes a very delicate juggling act in which setting priorities, budgeting time, and sharing the responsibilities of running a household are equally important considerations. Fortunately, it isn't often that we experience the type of absurd turn of events that occurred the month before we moved into a new home.

As Al and I were covering the Reagan and Carter campaigns in August, 1980, we found ourselves leaving notes for one another on the dining table, as we tried to reach decisions on paint colors. We took turns meeting the plumbers, electricians, and carpenter to discuss work needed on the house before we could move into it. Sometimes, our signals got crossed. I decided to cover a living room fireplace with a mirror, and thought I had Al's concurrence, until he walked in on a workman in the middle of constructing a dry wall, in preparation for the mirror.

"I had no idea you meant to hide the fireplace," Al told me, after practically dismissing the workman. "I thought you meant *on top of* it!" I realized then that I hadn't been very explicit, and apologized. But the confusion continued, as Al and I tried to cover the Democratic presidential nominating convention in New York, where, for one week, we supervised work on the house by long-distance.

Over Labor Day weekend, with an exquisitely poor sense of timing, we finally moved in. That Monday morning, we got up early, tired and sore from the move, drank a quick cup of coffee, and got into our respective cars, leaving a house cluttered with unpacked boxes and clothes and furniture in complete disarray. I was going to Andrews Air Force Base to follow the Carter campaign; Al, to Dulles Airport to pick up the Reagan entourage. A few blocks from home, we both stopped for a traffic light. Al leaned out the window and said, "This would make a great situation comedy." I didn't laugh very hard.

On normal working days we make a point of talking on the phone several times to keep each other aware of what the other is thinking or how the day is shaping up. We tell each other when the next few days are going to be hectic for one of us so that the other can pick up the slack and avoid taking on more than usual. Knowing what to expect from each other day to day and week to week goes a long way in heading off the inevitable disagreements that flare up in any marriage.

Of course, no marriage is completely fifty-fifty. I think the responsibilities of running a household weigh more heavily on women, whether they work outside the home or not, than on their husbands. But I think Al and I come as close as any couple to being equal partners in matters of home maintenance. Since I enjoy cooking more than Al does, I usually prepare the meals, and he scours the pots and pans and takes out the garbage. But on a night when I'm working late, he tries to make dinner, whether it's hamburgers or some frozen prepared dish or Chinese take-out. I'm in charge of learning how complicated video equipment works, since Al is not much for mechanical undertakings. But he knows more about automobiles than I do, so he takes care of getting the cars to the mechanic and making sure we have the requisite lube jobs and tire changes. When company is coming, we take turns preparing hors d'oeuvres, and Al mixes drinks and helps me serve and clear the table. We both try to keep the house neat between weekly visits from our housekeeper.

This sharing is essential to our relationship. At a Hunter College conference this year on "Women, Work, and Family," Dr. Lenora Cole-Alexander, director of the Labor Department's Women's Bureau, noted that although two-career families constitute 52 percent of all marriages, in only 12 percent of the households do the husband and wife share equally in chores and duties. "Maybe it's because of tradition," she explained to the *New York Times.* "Women have always done the cooking and the sewing and the cleaning." That's one tradition we don't need.

I have learned to make tradeoffs in budgeting my time. Al is very organized and is always reminding me to organize my time better. He makes lists of things he must do—errands, household chores, reading—even on the weekends. Without them, he says he would never get anything done. I used to resist because I didn't want all the spontaneity gone from my life. My workday and week is so regimented that I wanted to keep one corner of my life unstructured. But we've come closer to a meeting of the minds on this because I've found that the aggravation of unfinished tasks weighs heavily on me. I've concluded that it's better to plan my Saturday morning around grocery shopping and errand–running than having these tasks hanging over my head all weekend.

Because work defines so much of our lives, I think we are more acutely aware than many couples of needing time together and making that time when we need it, whether it's playing tennis, curling up on the sofa to watch TV, or enjoying a relaxing dinner for two at home. I also think we enjoy the simple pleasures of just being alone together more, judging from what I read about the number of couples who grow bored with each other. It just may be that despite the stringent demands of combining career and marriage, having separate, busy lives prolongs the courtship.

Or perhaps another way of looking at it is that there is a fine line between having enough time together and having too much time. Fortunately, we don't have to worry about the latter. And for us, making time for each other is really just a matter of sensitivity and seizing the opportunities. Couples who spend more time at home than we do may feel the need to get away for the night or the weekend in order to unwind. We prefer just staying home, or taking a drive in the country, or having a leisurely breakfast in bed.

We also like to laugh a lot together and are not exactly averse to playing childlike games. Whether it's this sort of frivolity or watching a football game, discussing movies or even clothes, there are distractions from our everyday focus on interest rates, the president's congressional relations, or international tensions. These lighter moments are as essential as they are enjoyable for us. Last year in a long article, the *Wall Street Journal* noted the growing joylessness in the twenty-five million two-paycheck families. A major reason: an inability to forget workday situations and decompress into a comfortable family life at home. Some of these households, noted psychiatrist Jay Rohrlich, may be run efficiently, but that "misses the point of what a home should be. You shouldn't be spontaneous, emotional and irrational if you're running Morgan Guaranty, but that's what a home life should be able to incorporate." Still, he noted, many "high-powered people are unhappy unless they are talking about high-powered issues. Talking about what's for dinner or a new dress is too trivial.

They're avoiding the real stuff of life." We certainly spend time talking about "high-powered issues," but we rarely avoid those "trivial" matters that are the "real stuff of life."

Time, of course, is a precious commodity, so most of our nonworking hours we spend together. I'm not big on bridge games or lengthy shopping sprees, and Al has little interest in hunting trips or poker games. With notable exceptions for old friends, I rarely spend a lot of time with "the girls," and Al hardly ever goes drinking with "the boys."

Recognizing how important balance is to our marriage made the decision to have a baby a question of upsetting that balance, as I think it is for most couples. Some may worry about whether a baby will strain the limits of the family budget, or the ability to meet the needs of older siblings. We wondered how we would fit a baby into our already-busy lives, and how our demanding and often erratic careers would affect a child.

And yet, we both knew from the start that we wanted a family. Perhaps it was a subconscious yearning to fulfill our biological destinies. Perhaps it was simply recognizing that, despite our concerns about the responsibilities involved in becoming parents, we have so much to give. We also knew from the beginning that because of our ages—I was thirty-three when we married and Al was thirty-seven—we couldn't postpone children for very long. So, as we settled into our second year of marriage, a baby was very much on our minds.

Jeffrey Woodruff Hunt

At one time, conventional wisdom in the television world held that women could not combine a successful reporting career with having children. Ten years ago, for example, Barbara Walters said the only reason she felt she could raise her young daughter at the same time she was co-anchoring the "Today" show was the relative stability of her daily work.

"I would not want to be a correspondent," she said. "I could not travel all over the country at this point in my life."

Walters, I think, spoke for a majority of women in television in the '70s. My first break in television news, of course, was in 1970, when I was hired to replace a woman who had quit her local reporting job at Atlanta's WAGA-TV to have a baby. But as women became more commonplace in television newsrooms, the rules seemed to change. Additionally, as more women entered other equally demanding professional fields, having a baby was considered no more upsetting to a woman's career than taking a few month's leave of absence was to a man's.

But while I *knew* all that, I was still apprehensive on Valentine's Day, 1981, when my doctor told me I was pregnant. My God, I thought, *This Is It*. I knew that my colleague, Lesley Stahl of CBS, had a three-year-old daughter and that Carole Simpson and Ann Compton of ABC had managed successfully to cover Congress while raising young children, but

I wondered how I would do it. As it turned out, those doubts were gradually erased by the anticipation and overwhelming emotion I felt as my baby's birth approached.

On the way home from the doctor's office that Saturday afternoon I calmly finished my errands, stopping at the grocery store and dry cleaner's. Perhaps I was subconsciously trying to demonstrate to myself that my life really wasn't going to change. My last stop was the drugstore, where I bought a card that said, "Happy Valentine's Day, Daddy." I signed it "from both of us." Of course, Al was delighted.

In our decision to start a family, timing was critical. Many people consider such things as their financial situation or the size of their house before they embark on parenthood; Al and I considered the dates of congressional recesses, likely presidential travel plans, and election years. Considering those factors, 1981 seemed like a vintage year for having a baby. Since it was the first year after a presidential election, there was sure to be a natural lull as the newly elected president settled in for his political honeymoon. In 1980, after the November election, Al began saying to me, "You know, there's never going to be a better time than now."

I also felt that I had reached a point in my career where I was on solid ground and no longer spending most of my time scurrying to catch up with other reporters. Although the assignment still carried with it long hours and unpredictable demands, after four years at the White House I felt myself settling into a natural working rhythm, if not exactly a preordained schedule. For the first time, I felt that I could afford to take a few months' maternity leave without worrying about missing something.

The most fundamental reason was that *we* felt we were ready to share the duties of child raising. That both Al and I believed we could adjust our professional and social schedules as we comfortably adjusted to new priorities.

But there was never any question that I would resume my assignment at the White House after our baby's birth. And after the critical first three months of my pregnancy, I phoned NBC's Washington bureau chief, Sid Davis, and the president of NBC News, Bill Small, to tell them the happy news and reassure them of my intention to return to work. My sense was that any employer, out of pragmatism if nothing else, worries whether motherhood is going to detract from a woman's commitment to and enthusiasm for her job. But I found that this, too, apparently has changed with the times. Davis, the father of two teenagers, told me to take as much time after the baby came as I wanted, and even telephoned Al to underscore his and NBC's support and understanding. Small, who can be a gruff news executive, turned out to be a real softie when it comes to children and family; he was as supportive as he was genuinely excited.

This support was important as, perhaps because I didn't know better, I was certain I could combine a family and career without cheating either. I even was reinforced by various studies, such as a recent one done of graduates of Columbia University's Business School. The survey of eighty graduates, from the late 1960s and early 1970s, equally divided between men and women of comparable backgrounds, suggested a family wasn't much of a deterrent to women's careers. About 65 percent of the women making over $50,000 were married and about two-thirds of them had children. Married women with children were doing about as well as single women or men. Further, Liz Roman Gallese of the *Wall Street Journal* surveyed eighteen of what she wrote were the "most ambitious" of these women, presumably in their early thirties. Almost half of these women had children; one had three kids. Their careers were flourishing. Professional success, Ms. Gallese concluded, hinges far more on a woman's own talents and drive than her family situation.

As for the more important point of being a good mother, while working, studies attesting to the quality of parenthood are elusive, if not impossible. Still, my instincts told me there was no way we ever would subordinate our parental responsibilities or affections. Further, I looked about and saw enough successful role models in Washington—career women who clearly were very competent and loving mothers—that I had little doubt that our course was eminently achievable.

From the start, my primary concern during my pregnancy was the health of our baby. If my doctor had suggested that working while pregnant posed a risk, I would have taken an immediate leave of absence. But fortunately, that possibility never arose. Aside from my needing more rest, the major side effect of my pregnancy was my growing girth. And even that didn't pose a problem until I was well along.

Much has been made about pregnant women's battle of the bulge on television. With more women on the air and more women choosing to work throughout their pregnancies, the question of how to photograph them inevitably arose. Do you cut them above the waist to conceal their condition? Or do you show their pregnancy and even allow them to discuss it on the air, as did anchorwoman Natalie Jacobson of Boston's WCVB-TV? During her pregnancy, Jacobson and her co-anchor and husband, Chet Curtis, used to make on-camera chit chat about her condition. Viewers patricipated in a count-down toward the baby's birth.

I think the question whether to show or not to show on the air really comes down to the kind of television program on which the pregnant woman appears. If I were the host of a talk show, a more informal and personable format, I would have no problem appearing pregnant on the air, as did Joan Lunden of ABC's "Good Morning America." But on a straight newscast I felt that showing my pregnancy on camera would distract from what I was saying. My closing stand-ups are often the critical part of my reports, driving home the point of the story. I didn't want viewers shouting across the living room, "Hey, look Alice, Judy Woodruff is going to have a baby!" I wanted viewers to listen to what I was saying.

When she was pregnant ABC's Ann Compton was reminded by the producer of "World News Tonight" of the "Elbow Rule"—"We don't want to see your elbows (on the air) until the baby is born." But I never discussed with NBC management whether to show my expanding profile on the air. Each television crew that rotated through White House coverage asked me, "Where do you want us to cut you off on camera?" I suggested they break me at the midriff, slightly higher than they normally would. Occasionally, for longer stand-ups, they used a wider angle lens and then zoomed in, rather than staying on a static shot. But even then, because they shot me straight-on, my pregnancy wasn't noticeable to viewers. The only inkling most people had of my great expectation was an Associated Press feature story on television's attitude toward showing pregnant women on the air. The story appeared in newspapers around the country.

Some friends and viewers urged me to show my pregnancy on the air, insisting that I would become a role-model for working expectant mothers. What's more, they argued, if more newswomen were shown pregnant, it might no longer be considered a distraction. But I didn't become pregnant to make a political or social statement.

As rare as pregnant women are in television news, they are even more of a novelty at the White House. I was surprised to find conversation among career women teetering between the Administration's budget proposals and nursery furnishings when my good friend Helen Thomas, UPI's White House correspondent, threw a baby shower for me. And I found the mostly male White House press corps and staff so solicitous of me that I sometimes wondered whether they were more anxious for the baby's arrival than I was—if only because they worried that one of them might be unexpectedly called on to midwife. Always willing to lend a hand, ABC's Sam Donaldson allayed that concern by volunteering to drive me to the hospital or serve as honorary White House midwife, as the need arose. But I had heard enough about the arrival of first babies to know that there is usually plenty of advance warning. If I started to go into labor at the White House, I intended to leave work and rush home or to the hospital. I had no intention of being a martyr.

Of course, some days during my pregnancy were less comfortable than others—for both of us. The baby always seemed to kick during briefings by the deputy press secretary, Larry Speakes, but never during those by Speakes' boss, David Gergen, the assistant to the President for White House communications. And I remember one particularly hot July day when, as I stood on the baking black asphalt driveway for nearly two hours staking out the southwest gate, my legs ached so badly that I finally had to sit on the curb. Seeing me perched there, a kindly uniformed security man walked over and invited me to sit inside the air-conditioned guards' booth. For a fleeting second, I was tempted. But, I didn't want special treatment, and I knew that it would take me that much longer to dash out to the waiting cars from the booth. Since I wasn't very fast on my feet then, I worried that I might miss the chance to question the congressmen for whom I was waiting as they emerged from the Oval Office.

I didn't miss any work during pregnancy, except for one weekend trip that President Reagan made at the beginning of September. It was my doctor's recommendation. In my eighth month, I accompanied Reagan on part of his month-long August vacation in California. Just in case, I mapped out ahead of time the location of hospitals, and collected names of recommended doctors in the Santa Barbara area. Al made the trip to cover the President for the *Journal,* so I was well looked-after.

The highlight of that trip—for everyone but me—was Reagan's visit to the aircraft carrier U.S.S. *Constellation.* The fifty or so reporters who accompanied the President were shuttled from shore to ship by Navy Cargo helicopters. The Navy hadn't counted on one of those reporters being eight months pregnant, and in a panic they insisted that the White House press staff stop me from going. To their credit (and perhaps thinking about their network coverage that night), the White House refused, telling the Navy that pregnancy wasn't a justification for preventing a legitimately accredited news-woman from covering a story.

As it turned out, the helicopter ride was the least of it. The deafening display of aerial maneuvers by F-14 fighter planes was something else. When the first of several sonic booms exploded, I was inside the ship and unprepared for the noise. I thought we had been accidentally bombed. I let out a scream, and the young ensign who was with me turned white. "Don't worry, don't worry," he said. I believe he thought I was going to have the baby right there.

My last day as a pregnant White House correspondent turned out to be so hectic that I didn't recognize the signs of impending labor. I began that morning with a visit to my doctor. He told me, "The baby is very low and could come any time. I'm not at all sure you're going to make it until the end of the month." But I didn't realize how prescient my doctor's prediction was.

That Tuesday, September 15, was a busy one for the President, which meant that it was a busy one for me, too. More than two dozen congressional leaders came to call on him to discuss Social Security assistance. Several business leaders had also been invited to a meeting with Reagan. And Ed Meese was up on the Hill lobbying for the Administration's proposed sale of AWAC radar planes to Saudi Arabia. We needed all three of us who were working at the White House for NBC that day in order to cover all the developing news.

I began to feel uncomfortable shortly after I arrived at my press-room cubicle that morning. But not enough so that I believed the time was close. Still, I didn't feel up to standing out on the driveway for hours, so I asked the other two NBC reporters, Emery King and Dave Rush, to cover the stakeouts of Oval Office visitors while I stayed in my chair, working the telephone. With all the news that day, I worked down to the wire putting together my report for "Nightly." It was after six when I finished taping my closing stand-up on the White House lawn. At the last minute, the producer cut my close without telling me, because the piece was running too long. Although I'm used to the frustrations of working within a minute-and-a-half time frame, that day the trimming of my closing was particularly irritating because I was so tired.

It was past seven when I left the White House to join Al and my agent, Ralph Mann, for drinks. Afterwards, Al and I dined at a neighborhood restaurant. We arrived home a little past ten-thirty, and I began getting ready for bed. I was brushing my teeth when I started to go into labor.

All I could think was that nothing was ready. I hadn't bought the layette yet. The nursery wasn't finished. My suitcase wasn't even packed.

Al phoned the doctor, who told us to drive directly to Georgetown Hospital, about five minutes away.

For several weeks I had known it was likely that I would require a cesarean delivery. My doctor had detected a possible problem on my last sonogram, which is a "sound picture" of the unborn baby normally used to determine the baby's position in the womb. After weeks of natural childbirth classes and practicing our Lamaze breathing exercises, Al and I were disappointed. But we agreed with the doctor that it was best to take every precaution.

At about quarter past two Wednesday morning, I was wheeled into the delivery room with Al at my side. Having him there eased my nervousness and made us feel closer than ever. We teased each other about whether it would be a boy or a girl. I tended toward wanting a son, probably because I had always longed for a brother. Al was rooting for a daughter. I won. At 2:57 A.M. on September 16, I felt a pull as the doctor announced, "You have a wonderful baby boy."

The announcement was trumpeted by loud, lusty cries. Moments later, Al took our son from the nurse to show him to me. I could hardly believe that all those flutters and kicks I had felt in my womb added up to this little person. Tears of joy streamed down both our cheeks as we saw for the first time our baby's round little red face.

Now that we had a son, we agreed that I would pick the name from among the three or four possibilities we had selected. My top two choices were Andrew and Jeffrey. On my way to the recovery room, Al asked, "Is his name Andrew?" But I was too excited at that point to make up my mind. When Al brought the baby to my room a couple of hours later, he pressed me for a decision. "The other kids in the nursery are making fun of him, calling him No Name Baby," he said. "You have to name him now."

"All right," I said, my eyes fixed on the cherubic face belonging to the blanket-wrapped bundle. "He's Jeffrey."

Jeffrey Woodruff Hunt's first day in the world was a media blitz. My office passed the news on to the "Today" show, which announced Jeffrey's arrival on the air. That afternoon, an NBC camera crew showed up to photograph me holding our son. Al had warned me to expect them, but said it was just for the family photo album. That evening, Jeffrey appeared on "Nightly News" with John Chancellor. Chancellor told me later that it was the first time he could remember in his twenty years with NBC that the newscast carried the announcement of the normal birth of a baby who was not related to either a President or royalty.

"How are you going to explain to the kid that his whole life was downhill from his first week?" joked Al's boss, Fred Taylor, the executive editor of the *Wall Street Journal*. "Wait until he's two or three before he starts doing stand-uppers in front of the White House!"

After Chris Wallace made an announcement on the "Today" show, the phone rang throughout the day with calls from well-wishers, and I was dazed by both excitement and exhaustion that night when Al handed me the telephone—again.

"It's the President calling," he said.

"The president of what?" I asked groggily.

"The President of the United States. He wants to speak with you."

Sure enough, the caller was Ronald Reagan. "Nancy and I want to congratulate you," he said. "How are you feeling?"

"Oh, I feel fine, Mr. President," I answered weakly.

He laughed. "Well you don't sound like it."

"It all happened so fast," I said.

"It always does. Nancy and I had been to a horse show just before our first one came along. She almost had to be taken to the hospital in an ambulance."

Jeffrey didn't meet the President until two months later, when I took him to the White House to show him off to my friends in the press office and press corps. Of course, Jeffrey quickly became the center of attention. As we entered the press briefing room, Larry Speakes was only too happy to interrupt his grilling by reporters on the scandal involving then-national security advisor Richard Allen. Like a drowning man being thrown a life preserver, Speakes seized the occasion. "Jeffrey!" he exclaimed, motioning us to the podium.

I had hoped for a chance to sneak Jeffrey in with a pack of reporters to witness a Presidential photo opportunity or ceremony. But I was caught totally off guard when an aide told me that the President wanted an audience with my son. So was Jeffrey, who had just finished a bottle.

The aide led me down the hallway to the Oval Office where Al, whom the White House had phoned minutes earlier, was waiting for us. As we stood outside the President's door, waiting, Jeffrey began to fuss. I realized that I hadn't burped him after his feeding. "Al," I said, "quick! run and get the towels I left in the press room."

Al had no sooner walked out when David Fischer, the President's special assistant, appeared, ready to escort us into the Oval Office. I had a problem. I couldn't keep the President waiting, but I had to burp Jeffrey.

"Can't you wait just a minute?" I asked, trying to stall until Al returned with the towels. Just then, Al came running down the hall and Fischer ushered us in to see the President.

Reagan rose from behind his oversized, mahogany desk and walked over to greet us. "How are you?" he said, shaking Al's hand. He smiled at me and then peered down at Jeffrey, who still had not been burped.

"What a handsome little guy," Reagan said. "Here, let me have him." As he reached for the baby, I looked at Al and held my breath, certain that our son was about to spit up on the President of the United States.

There are some people who seem awkward when holding a baby, and some who just warm to it naturally. Ronald Reagan is one of the latter. Jeffrey seemed to sense this, for the minute the President took him, he calmed down—to our relief. Of course, the bright flashes as the White House photographers began snapping pictures of the President holding Jeffrey may have helped.

"Jeffrey," said the President, bouncing the baby up and down, "when you get a little bigger, your father is going to sit you on his knee and tell you this nursery rhyme: 'This is the way the ladies ride, trim, trim, trim. This is the way the gentlemen ride, bim, bim, bim. This is the way the boogey man rides, boo, boo, boo.' "

Jeffrey became so excited that the pacifier fell out of his mouth and onto the floor near Reagan's feet. Instinctively, the President started to reach down for it, until an aide rushed over to retrieve it.

Al and I were becoming concerned that we might be wearing out our welcome by taking too much of the President's time. We thanked him, which is ordinarily the cue for the President's aides to hustle visitors out. But Reagan continued to chat and seemed reluctant to give up the baby, until Jeffrey began to squirm. As he handed the baby over to me, Reagan jokingly attributed Jeffrey's fussing to the fact that the photographers' flashes had stopped.

I'm not so naive as to think that Ronald Reagan would have spent ten minutes with my son if I were an obscure bus driver instead of NBC's White House correspondent. But I believe he found this time a welcome change of pace from his usual duties. He certainly seemed in no hurry to move on to his next visitor, the President of Sudan.

A few days later, Al suggested that it was important that Jeffrey learn early about the balance of powers in our system of government. "I don't want him to be the Hugh Sidey of babies," he said, referring to the *Time* magazine columnist who is often sympathetic to the White House point of view.

So when Al's day to look after Jeffrey coincided with an unusual weekend meeting of Congress because of a budget dispute, our son was introduced to Capitol Hill while his father covered the session. House Speaker Tip O'Neill, Senate Majority Leader Howard Baker, and Senate Budget Committee Chairman Pete Domenici all held and coddled Jeffrey. I doubt that his presence facilitated the legislative process, but it did provide politicians with an opportunity to practice their baby cuddling skills.

I stayed home for three months after Jeffrey was born. After talking to several friends, who also were working mothers, I felt it was important to savor those first months and I needed that much time with my baby. Much longer than three months, I worried, and I would get professionally restless.

As it turned out, learning to tailor my schedule to my son's needs, watching him grow and change from day to day, and discovering my instinctive abilities as a mother left little room for feeling restless about work. And although I continued to keep up with the news at the White House through the newspapers and evening newscasts, I found that my reading tastes expanded from titles such as *The Foundations of Modern Political Thought* to Dr. Spock.

Some women, I know, find those first months draining and confining, and become anxious about how much the baby dominates their thoughts, as well as their lives. I was warned by friends that I might find myself worrying that I was forgetting everything I had learned on the job and in the world outside, as I focused on such baby minutia as diaper rash and feeding schedules. But I was never aware of feeling depressed or anxious during my months at home caring for my baby. And even though this was the longest I had ever been away from work, I didn't worry that my mind was going stale. I welcomed this chance to learn about my baby and how to care for him, and found it no small intellectual challenge.

This challenge clearly was facilitated by the considerable

help I had from our nanny, Sabine Laborde, who came to live with us shortly after Jeffrey came home from the hospital. But I think it also has to do with the fact that Jeffrey was a planned and very much wanted baby. He came into my life at a time when I felt reasonably secure in my job, my career, my marriage, and myself. If there is a secret to managing career, motherhood and marriage, I believe that is it. And I feel very fortunate that I didn't have the pressures of an unhappy marriage or uncertain job hanging over my head—as many women do—at this critical time.

That same sense of security and stability, I also believe, helped tremendously when it came time for me to turn from being an at-home mother to being a working mother who was no longer the full-time caretaker of her infant. Sure, I felt the tugging at my heartstrings. But I also knew that while I was away my baby was being loved and cared for by a woman whom I had come to regard as a member of our family. There was never any doubt in my mind that he was happy and receiving the best of care.

There's no question that this kind of child care is expensive. But one of the compensating advantages of the long hours my job requires is that I'm paid enough to be able to afford it. And while experts naturally disagree on how much time a mother should spend with her child, I think there is a tendency to overestimate how much time she can be expected to spend with her child, whether she works outside the home or not.

As anthropologist Margaret Mead said, "You can't expect a mother to be with a small child all the time."

It also helped that I was able to make the transition from maternity leave to work by initially working part time at home as one of three contributors to an NBC documentary on Ronald Reagan's first year as President.

Al and I also recognize that we have more flexibility in our work schedules and opportunities for spending extended time with Jeffrey than many two career couples. When I had to spend several days in New York wrapping up my part of the documentary, Jeffrey and Sabine came with me. We intend to take our son along on the accommodating travel assignments, such as the President's vacations. When the President took a five-day working vacation in Barbados, Jeffrey and Al went with me; Al went, not as a journalist, but as a spouse and baby-sitter, and we spent some glorious hours together (when I wasn't working). And Al looks forward to those long Congressional recesses because they mean uninterrupted time with Jeffrey.

When I started back to work full time in early January, we carefully figured out how we would get up around 6:30 A.M. and take turns feeding, diapering and playing with him, while we both got ready for work. This worked beautifully for three days. On the fourth it all fell apart when the "Today" show phoned and said I had to come in at 6 A.M. to do a piece.

Al frantically rushed to fill the void that morning, waking the baby, watching me on television, changing the diapers, feeding Jeffrey breakfast, dressing him and himself. A bit exhausted by the time he got on the subway headed for his office, he nevertheless was feeling very proud of how well he had handled it all—until he looked down and saw he had on one black loafer and one brown loafer.

For the first two months after I went back to work, I managed to continue nursing Jeffrey. But that ended when I had to accompany President Reagan to California for a week in early March. I considered taking Jeffrey with me, but it seemed impossible during this trip. So I sought the advice of our pediatrician, who advised me that there was no medical reason to keep on breast feeding a five-month-old. I regretted having to relinquish the special bond with my son that I felt through nursing, but I felt fortunate to have been able to continue that long.

For me, one of the biggest advantages of being a working mother is that I don't worry about my son having a part-time father. It's all too easy for men, even a loving and sensitive one like Al, to shift the responsibility of parenting to women, particularly when those women are at home full-time. I think this is unfair to the mother and to the children, who I think need to feel that Dad is more than that fellow who takes them to the zoo on Sundays and occasionally metes out spankings. But I also think it's terribly sad for the fathers who never discover their capacity for nurturing.

Parents who both work, out of necessity if nothing else, are having to confront the shared responsibility of raising children. As a result, I think they are helping to change in a positive way attitudes about the role fathers play in their children's lives. Eventually, I hope we'll see the day when mothers will no longer be called upon to defend their decision to continue working any more than fathers are today. Neither will it be considered remarkable for a father to take a leave of absence from his job to raise his children, as ABC newsman Ted Koppel did while his wife attended law school. It's worth noting that Koppel's career didn't suffer, as evidenced by his position as anchorman of ABC's "Nightline" newscast. Perhaps because he is the son of a pediatrician and the eldest in a family of four, Al is as much interested in Jeffrey's development and care as I am. That doesn't mean that he cares less about his work, but it does mean that his priorities are shifting.

We don't for a moment think we're going to combine careers and a child without some difficulty and some sacrifice. Even during this first year, we find we go out less, see fewer movies and plays, and are more judicious about spending our extra time working or attending political gatherings. These trade-offs seem reasonable to us at this stage. For our interests and priorities have clearly shifted. We spend much more time thinking and talking about Jeffrey's development or sleeping and eating habits, or latest trick or cutest ploy, and comparatively less about the budget or El Salvador or the agenda of the New Right of the Republican party.

I'm still learning how to resolve the conflicts between baby and work. I don't delude myself that I'm the "superwoman" who can do both jobs—mother and reporter—equally well all the time. There is no happy solution for those evenings when I know my son is waiting to see me and I learn that I must stay to develop a late-breaking story until after he's gone to bed for the night. Those will be painful times. And I suspect that I will lose a little of my edge as a journalist on the days when Jeffrey comes down with a cold or some other childhood illness. As much as I will want to be with him, I may not always be able to.

I don't like to think about those day-to-day incidents in Jeffrey's young life that I won't be there to witness. At some of those moments there will be no substitute for an attendant parent. And I reluctantly realize that he may grow more dependent for a time on his stand-in "parent," Sabine, than on his mother and father. But on balance I also think that Jeffrey will come to understand that his parents' love for him is not diminished by their desire to seek fulfillment through their careers. He will know we are happier, more satisfied people because we made this choice. More by deed than by word, we hope to bring him to realize that the satisfaction and happiness we derive from our work will make us better parents.

Window Dressing on the Set?

When I applied for a job as a TV news reporter in 1969, the replies from station news directors around the country pretty much summed up the industry's attitude toward employing women then: "We're not looking for a woman," was the frequent refrain. "We're looking for a reporter." Actually that attitude eventually helped me to get my first reporting job at Atlanta's WQXI, where I was hired to fill a slot vacated by a woman having a baby. Still, there was a lot of hurt. "Well, I see you've hired another dumb blonde," a middle-aged reporter said to the news director after my hiring, I later learned. I thought—in many instances I knew—I was not taken as a serious news professional by many of the figures I covered, as well as by many of my colleagues in a male-dominated business.

Eight years later, however, when I had moved to a network job and was assigned to cover the Carter White House, women had come a long way. Aided by legal challenges to sex discrimination and a belated realization of the commercial value of women, TV stations and networks were actively looking for women reporters. The assignments were not only more plentiful but more diverse and better. Indeed, there was a certain irony here: In Atlanta, I struggled to overcome the dumb-blonde stereotype and prove I could do the job *even though* I was a woman; in Washington, I sometimes had to overcome the perception that I was assigned to the White House just *because* I was a woman.

To be sure, there are other problems, too. Double standards are still applied in salaries, assignments, and attitudes toward women reporters, and we are much more affected than our male counterparts by age discrimination. In Washington, the center of network news-gathering and the pinnacle of the news profession, women journalists remain a distinct minority. In his book *The Washington Reporters,* Stephen Hess surveyed the capitol's news corps (television and print) and found that as recently as 1978 male reporters outnumbered females four to one. At the same time, there were two male professionals for every female in the country at large. Since the 1978 ratio differed very little from that found in a national survey of journalists in 1971, Hess concluded: "It can be assumed that the hiring of female reporters in Washington lags behind the rest of the United States by seven years."

Also, I fear, stereotypes are slow to disappear. In a March 1982 *Washington Post* profile, White House Press Secretary Larry Speakes acknowledged that the President still had difficulty distinguishing between me and CBS's Lesley Stahl. Somehow, I doubt he has the same trouble with Sam Donaldson and John Palmer. But you know how it is: those blonde, female TV reporters all look alike. . . . My women friends who are reporters tell me the discrimination they've experienced covering official Washington outside the White House is alive and rampant even now, and especially at agencies peopled with men from technical or military backgrounds.

Yet the strides we've made are extraordinary. At all three networks, women are working as newscast anchors or morning show hosts or correspondents covering such heretofore male bastions as the Pentagon or such prestige beats as Congress, the State Department, the White House, or the national political scene. No doubt we still have a way to go, but it's a far cry from the early days of television when that first woman pioneer, Pauline Frederick, was struggling to break in.

Pauline Frederick's credentials were impressive for a man

or a woman. She was a political science major, took an advanced degree in international law, and had reported for the *Washington Star* and *U.S. News*. Actually, in the late 1940s, when many radio performers were trying to break into television, Frederick seized her chance by staying in radio. She figured that since all the men were fleeing to television she would have a better chance of getting on the air if she stayed put. In those days, the few women news broadcasters were largely barred from the air unless they had scoops.

Frederick's radio experience had already taught her a lot about double standards. She had tried to convince her superiors that she could broadcast news, only to be told that "listeners are going to tune out because a woman's voice doesn't carry authority." Years later Frederick wrote: "I'm terribly sorry that I didn't have courage enough in those days to tell him that I knew his wife's voice carried plenty of authority in his house." Nevertheless, one day Frederick's news director called her in and said he wanted her to switch to television. She said she didn't know what to do. "Don't worry," he said, "we don't either."

So Frederick joined ABC and became the first woman television correspondent—and quickly learned that getting on the tube with her stories wasn't any easier than getting on the radio had been. After her boss told her she would have a better chance at more air time if she covered a subject no one else was covering, Frederick carved out a beat for herself at the fledgling United Nations. But even becoming an expert was not enough to assure a newswoman an outlet in reporting on her subjects. Frederick learned about "directives from higher up" not to use her on the air unless she got exclusive stories. . ." Over a twenty-six-year career in television news, Frederick managed to get enough exclusives to distinguish herself as the only reporter ever ranked among the ten most admired women in the world by a Gallup Poll.

More than ten years passed before a second woman, who

also started in radio, was able to crack the all-male lineup of network television news correspondents. And when she did, Nancy Dickerson of CBS found getting on the tube with her stories no easier than Pauline Frederick had. In her autobiography, *Among Those Present,* Dickerson recalled that she never could have made it as a television correspondent during the early 1960s without scoring exclusives. Staying on top of the same stories the rest of the Washington press corps was following simply wasn't enough. "I realized," she wrote, "that the only way I could get on the air was to report news no one else had access to." But even then, Dickerson felt that her exclusive stories were often sidetracked to radio or minor television newscasts. And when they did make the evening news show, they were frequently worked into an anchorman's script without any credit being given to her. Among network executives—this was after she had shifted to NBC—Dickerson wrote that she suffered a women's lib backlash; suddenly men felt their masculinity threatened."

These problems were by no means limited to television journalists. My friend Helen Thomas of UPI wrote in her book *Dateline: White House* that in 1961 she was imploring foreign leaders to speak at the Women's National Press Club when they came to Washington, instead of at the more noted Washington Press Club, which excluded females. The National Press Club didn't admit women for another ten years.

As recently as a decade ago this view was reinforced by one of the more progressive men in the business—Reuven Frank, president of NBC News then and reappointed to that post early in 1982. "I have the strong feeling that audiences are less prepared to accept news from a woman's voice than from a man's," he said in an interview that caused barely a ripple.

In fairness, only a year and a half later Mr. Frank significantly modified his views: "People don't watch what they have to; they watch what they like," he explained in another interview. "I think they have now been conditioned—all of it is a process of conditioning and development—so that in reporting they will take [women in TV]. I don't know who's going to take the first chance on a woman in a major anchor position. It'll be interesting to find out." In April 1982, Frank told me an anchor person has to "take over the tube" to be successful. "You no longer assume women can't command the tube," he said, "we've passed that hurdle. But we still have a way to go . . . audiences are slow-moving beasts."

There is no doubt that Pauline Frederick and the other women in television in the 1960s were the pathfinders for all of us today. But quite apart from their skills, determination, and tenacity, women were assisted by some outside events, too. These included social, economic, and legal pressures that grew out of years of discriminatory hiring practices. Because of its increasingly prominent role and its dependence upon government licensing, television was an obvious target at a time when the country was rethinking what equality regardless of race, color, creed, and—yes, sex—really meant in American society. A lot of people thought it should mean equal opportunities in employment, which it obviously had not meant up to that time. And the result was the passage of the 1964 Civil Rights Act, which was amended to include women, and the formation of the Equal Opportunity Commission.

The public's heightened awareness of discrimination also gave rise to a number of concerned citizens' watchdog groups which challenged television's compliance with antidiscrimination laws. Since television by its very nature as a communications medium represents society, the feeling was that television should be an accurate reflection of society. So as a result of pressures from the public, which began challenging individual stations' and networks' broadcast licenses, the Federal Communications Commission issued an order prohibiting discrimination and requiring stations to file affirmative action programs with the agency. In 1971 the FCC added women to the list of minorities covered by the equal employment opportunity guidelines. The burgeoning numbers of women in television today, myself included, are to a great degree the result of that FCC ruling, which was, in turn, the result of public pressure, not the industry's largesse.

But there were commercial considerations as well. Television networks finally came to realize that not only were women not a liability but, in some instances, a valuable asset in attracting viewers. According to the A. C. Nielsen Company Television Rating Service, women are heavier TV viewers than men. More importantly, almost every available survey suggests that in recent years the public has come to accept professional women about as readily as it does our male counterparts. This isn't limited to TV news. A Boston University study, for example, concluded that the public actually had slightly *more* confidence in official spokeswomen for government agencies and large corporations than it did in spokesmen. Other studies have demonstrated the public's preference for newswomen over newsmen. Prior to hiring Barbara Walters as co-anchor for its evening news show, ABC surveyed its viewers and found that 46 percent preferred a female newscaster, compared to 41 percent who had no sexual preference and 13 percent who preferred a male. A 1974 survey by the Screen Actors' Guild found that 67 percent of the respondents wanted to see women in positions of authority on television.

I'm not sure I totally accept the validity of these surveys; others, I suspect, might show a preference for males in some respects. The point, though, is that the long-held notion that women wouldn't be accepted as authority figures disseminating information plainly doesn't hold today.

All of these changes undoubtedly helped me. I was hired as a news secretary at Atlanta's WAGA in the spring of 1968— just three years before the FCC ruling went into effect. But in those three years the attitude toward and opportunities for women had shifted more than it seemed they had in the last century.

When I entered the TV news business after four years of college, the only opportunity for me was to become a secretary. Although this wasn't quite the job I had gone to college to prepare for, I reasoned that I had to start somewhere, and resolved to work my way up to reporter. I quickly came to realize it wasn't quite that simple. "We already have a woman reporter," the news director told me. And when I pointed out that she covered women's features and I meant to cover hard news, he looked at me as though this was the most absurd thing he had ever heard. Months later, he promoted me to weekend weathergirl.

The idea that one woman reporter was all a station needed was by no means limited to Atlanta local television, however. I learned that when I applied to TV news directors around the country who had posted available reporting jobs in *Broadcasting* magazine.

When I was hired as a reporter in 1970—a year before the FCC guidelines went into effect, but with stations already feeling the pressure to hire more women—my employers made it clear they were looking for a woman to replace a woman. If I had been a white male, I wouldn't have gotten that job. But I did get the job. And I advanced. I was made a co-anchor on the noon news, as well as on the evening news for a period. And I was assigned to cover the most prestigious political beat, the state legislature, for the entire five years I worked as a local reporter. My employers gave me the opportunities to succeed, as they did other women they hired during the same period. Whatever their motives, their policies helped me. So much so, that when I began to look for a job in a larger market or at a network, one news executive told me he was sorry he had no openings but felt that with my "obvious ability and experience," I would soon be offered the job I wanted. He may have been flattering me, but certainly the years I spent at WAGA in Atlanta were a considerable asset.

Once inside NBC, I did at first experience frustrations in attempting to advance. But this was due more to inexperience in covering a national political campaign than to any discrimination because of my sex. Catherine Mackin was used heavily in NBC's political coverage in 1976, as was Lesley Stahl at CBS. And when NBC offered me the position of White House correspondent in December 1976, I had been with the network less than two full years. I had worked to win the confidence of my superiors, but they made a leap of faith in giving me one of the most important breaks of my career. Now, as a very visible veteran of five years of reporting on the presidency, it would be hard for me to argue that I've suffered discrimination because of my sex. And others in the industry have made gains at the same time. From being only two out of more than forty news correspondents at each of the three networks in 1970, women constituted 10 percent of the network reporting staffs in 1977. At NBC that figure had grown to almost 20 percent by early 1982.

The most progress has come in the more visible positions. From 1964, when Marlene Sanders of ABC became the first female network anchor, filling in for a male colleague for a brief period, to the early 1980s, when every network has at least one woman serving as a co-anchor, women have come a long way. Barbara Walters is the only woman ever to have regularly anchored a weekday evening news program, but many other women have been placed in important anchor positions. On ABC, Sylvia Chase has co-anchored the Saturday evening news, and Sandy Hill and, later, Joan Lunden, have served as co-hosts on the "Good Morning America" program. On NBC, Catherine Mackin anchored the Sunday evening news in the mid-1970s, and she was succeeded by Jessica Savitch, who now anchors the Saturday "Nightly News." Jane

Pauley also anchored one of NBC's weekend news programs, in addition to serving as co-host of the "Today" show, and Linda Ellerbee co-anchors "NBC News Overnight." Meanwhile, at CBS the "Morning News" has used a succession of women co-anchors, including Sally Quinn, Lesley Stahl, and, most recently, Diane Sawyer.

Women have made equally visible progress at local stations. In almost every sizable city in the country there is a woman co-anchoring the news. And some of them are among the highest paid people in the business. Connie Chung with KNXT in Los Angeles reportedly earns well over half a million dollars a year.

What is just as significant, women are being assigned to more prestigious beats than ever before. Cassie Mackin, then with NBC, and perhaps the most prominent woman network reporter in the 1970's, became the first female reporter at the 1972 political conventions. In 1982, five of the ten network correspondents covering the White House are women. They are Ann Compton of ABC, Lesley Stahl and Deborah Potter at CBS, and Andrea Mitchell and me at NBC. Diane Sawyer, who now co-anchors the "CBS Morning News," earned a glittering reputation as a reporter while assigned to the State Department. Even the male-dominated Pentagon was recently covered for a brief time by a woman—Hilary Brown, when she worked for NBC. (Incidentally, Hilary is one of several women correspondents who have earned their stripes by covering the battlefield. She worked in the Middle East in the late 1970s; Robin Wright of CBS covered conflict on the African continent during the same period; and Liz Trotta covered Southeast Asia for NBC in the early 1970s). Capitol Hill is also populated with its share of women television reporters: Marya McLaughlin and Susan Spencer for CBS, Lisa Myers for NBC, and, in earlier years, Carole Simpson, Linda Ellerbee, Jessica Savitch, and Catherine Mackin for NBC, and Ann Compton for ABC.

A survey of Washington reporters in 1978 showed that few of these women complained about their positions. Stephen Hess noted in *The Washington Reporters* that, by and large, women employed by the prestige news organizations (i.e., the networks) did not feel discriminated against. "They identify you with your organization, not your gender," one respondent told Hess. Although there are no easily obtainable statistics on the subject, just looking around the network newsrooms reveals that more women are being used as field producers: Dina Modianot and Susan LaSalla of NBC, Sharon Young of ABC, and Rita Braver and Susan Zirinsky of CBS are among the best in the business. Behind the scenes, women dominate the Sunday interview shows: Joan Barone produces CBS's "Face the Nation," and Betty Dukert produces NBC's "Meet the Press." The higher one looks on the executive ladder, the fewer women there are, but progress has been made. Several women have become news program producers, and women are used frequently in the less powerful job of production assistant.

At the highest management levels, advancement has been slow, but it has come. A landmark survey on women and minorities in broadcasting, done by the U.S. Commission on Civil Rights in 1977, and entitled *Window Dressing on the Set,* reported that there had been no significant increase over a two-year period in the percentages of women employed as officials and managers, and summed up the situation by saying, "White males continue to hold the vast majority" of the executive positions at the networks and the local stations. But a check with the Radio and Television News Directors' Association in early 1982 reveals that the number of women news directors at the 473 commercial television stations around the country grew from only 2 in 1972 to more than 30 in 1979. Also in 1982 at least four of the network news bureau chiefs for NBC were women: Rebecca Bell in Paris, Elda Guglilmetti in Rome, Frieda Morris in Chicago, and Ellen McKeefe in

New York. In addition, each of the networks has at least one woman vice-president in its news division.

The future seems almost certain to bring more and more women into the upper echelons and the front ranks of network news. Women now outnumber men, 38,000 to 30,000, in the nation's journalism schools, according to Jeani Wilson, a graduate student at the University of Michigan. Wilson is conducting a comprehensive survey of the status of women in television news and fears that some of the obvious strides women have made may disappear. In her travels around the country and in interviews with women at every level of the business and with the executives who hire them, Wilson senses that pressure to promote women is decreasing. She believes that without continued impetus from the EEOC, the Federal Communications Commission, and the women's movement (which has been preoccupied in recent years with the fight to win ratification of the Equal Rights Amendment), news directors and network executives may lose some of their incentive to hire and promote women.

It would be foolish to deny that even in a time of progress there aren't residual problems. Take, for instance, the reaction when Barbara Walters was hired as the first regular network anchorwoman in 1976. ABC awarded her a five-year, million-dollar-a-year contract. This lucrative figure was roundly denounced as marking the beginning of a show-business atmosphere and the end of professional integrity in TV news. Walter Cronkite, who was then earning less than a million dollars a year as an anchor, described his reaction to a CBS affiliates' conference: "There was a first wave of nausea, the sickening sensation that we were going under, that all of our efforts to hold network television news aloof from show business had failed." A CBS executive suggested, "This isn't journalism, this is a minstrel show. Is Barbara Walters a journalist or is she Cher?" It had nothing to do with her sex, these gentlemen insisted; it was all a matter of principle.

But then four years later CBS annointed Dan Rather to succeed Cronkite as anchorman of the "Evening News." His reported contract: almost $10 million over five years, twice what Walters was paid and considerably more even after adjusting for inflation. And what did these gentlemen say then? Was Walter Cronkite nauseated by his successor's salary? Or did the CBS executive worry whether Dan Rather was a journalist or Sonny Bono? Funny, but we didn't hear a peep from them on Mr. Rather's salary.

Ironically, in his autobiography, *The Camera Never Blinks,* Rather himself expressed serious misgivings about whether any journalist should be paid so much money. Writing four years before he succeeded Cronkite, Rather addressed Barbara Walter's salary: "If anyone comes close to being worth a million, she may. But in my own view no one in this business is, no matter what or how many shows they do, unless they find a cure for cancer on the side."

There may be subtle discrimination in the matter of appearances, too. While few of us are ravishing beauties, physical attractiveness is a more important factor in hiring and promoting women in television than it is for men. You see very few fat, balding women on the air. Despite the stereotype of the blow-dried TV reporter (all too true in some local markets), many of my male colleagues are no threat to Paul Newman. I am often asked, Do you have to be blonde to get ahead in TV news? Witness, people say, Diane Sawyer, Jessica Savitch, Cassie Mackin, Lesley Stahl, and me—all blondes. In candor, it probably helps. Yet it certainly hasn't hindered Barbara Walters, Ann Compton, Andrea Mitchell, and others, none of whom are blonde.

I suspect salary discrimination persists, too. It's not much of a secret that, down the line, women usually aren't paid quite as well as their male peers. I remember that when I was anchoring two local news shows in Atlanta at the same time I was denied a $50-a-week raise by the station manager. With a straight face he explained: "You're making a nice salary for a girl." My male co-anchor, meanwhile, was making $6,000 a year more than I was. I really don't feel slighted by our salaries in television; we are handsomely rewarded and I'm making a bigger salary than I ever dreamed of. But it simply isn't acceptable that our male counterparts still do even better.

Moreover, if we don't suffer from strict sex discrimination women do seem subject to age discrimination. This is undoubtedly a problem that reaches beyond TV news, but it's especially vivid in our very visible business. Many men reach their career peaks in their mid-forties; graying temples and character lines etched in their faces seem to provide an air of sagacious maturity. Unfortunately, the same view isn't held about women. Quite the contrary. When we reach our mid-forties, the networks start thinking about sending us out to pasture. In August 1981 *New York* magazine ran an article entitled, "TV News and the Older Woman." Middle-aged women, it found, are almost invisible on TV news. As I mentioned before, most local TV stations around the country have women anchors or co-anchors. And yet, as I travel around, I notice that the vast majority appear to be in their twenties or thirties. On the network level, you can count on one hand the number of women in their mid-forties or over who appear regularly on the air.

CBS anchor Dan Rather conceded as much in the *New York* piece. "There is no joy in admitting there is a prejudice against women of a certain age," he was quoted as saying. But "it is sad and it is a fact that it's very difficult for women past forty to make it on the air. If a woman establishes herself young enough, the odds are still strongly against her staying on the air. But the really discouraging thing is that women who don't have much network exposure or local anchoring experience by forty have no chance at all. Television is a youth business and women feel this more than men." Then there was the cited case of a woman applying for a job with a CBS bureau chief who praised her credentials but warned that she should remember she would be over the hill at thirty-five.

This age barrier may be the most significant hurdle women still face in television news. It is more than just a disadvantage; it is the final litmus test of our acceptability to the industry and the public. If we're hired primarily because we're pretty and young, we will be put out to pasture once the wrinkles emerge. But if we're hired because we're good reporters, tough interviewers, insightful judges of news, and polished broadcasters, then we will grow—gray or not—more authoritative and better appreciated as we reach our forties and fifties. My own view is that the times are changing, and networks will find it much tougher to farm out many of us when we pass forty. We are a pushier, more assertive breed that isn't going to take that treatment quietly. And the marketing types will discover that older women aren't really a disadvantage, just as a decade ago they belatedly found out that younger women could be as appealing as men. Among other factors, they will realize it's economically inefficient to invest all that time and money in us and then lose our services in our most productive years.

Of course, I would feel more comfortable about this if there were more women news executives. If the networks really want to make greater strides here, some extra effort is necessary. For in our business as in others some unfortunate tensions between male managers and women subordinates impede the advancement of women in management jobs. At least one company in another field, Continental Illinois National Bank & Trust Company, tried to address this problem directly a few years ago. It established a development program to deal with communications problems between male managers and women subordinates after it discovered that, while women were coming in at the entry level in sufficient numbers, they weren't rising, largely because many of the company's men didn't want them to. The bank wanted the men to realize that most of the women had the same ambitions, goals, feelings, and frustrations about their careers as they did. The program shows promise. It was reported that last year 21 percent of the bank's middle management executives were women, double the percentage of five years earlier. I'm not sure we can duplicate that kind of program in TV news, but clearly some special attention is necessary in this area.

Unfortunately, there are still some men, albeit now a distinct minority, who can't stand the idea of working with or against a woman. Somehow it threatens their masculinity. This is a rapidly diminishing breed, thank goodness. None of the men I have worked closely with in recent years—John Palmer, Bill Lynch, John Dancy, or Emery King, all of NBC—or worked against—including Bill Plante, Sam Donaldson, Bob Schieffer, and Bob Pierpoint—have ever exhibited these traits. That's encouraging, because the old argument that we're somehow crowding men out of opportunities is exaggerated. Nobel Prize-winning economist Paul Samuelson summed it up almost ten years ago in testimony before the Congressional Joint Economic Committee. "The gains that come to living standards in national income by additional productivity of a new group, i.e., women, are not at the expense of previous groups in society," Dr. Samuelson testified. "No man's masculinity is really going to be threatened and his paycheck is not going to be threatened. This kind of effect that I am speaking of has been demonstrated again and again by the history of U.S. immigration, by the long overdue upgrading of black Americans' economic opportunities, and by the increasing education of all classes of American society."

The argument can also be made that, sometimes, women in television news have been their *own* worst enemies. Because there are so few of us in the upper echelons, we're compared to one another and, more often than is necessary, we compete against each other. All too often I've seen women measure themselves by how well they outdo one another, rather than ignoring sex differences and competing with those reporters— male *or* female—who are doing the same jobs they are. Perhaps it's a holdover from the years when we were told that there was only one woman's slot. Whatever the reason, it's unnecessary.

There is a special responsibility I feel women in television news have: to be role models for millions of women who were raised to think of themselves as second-class citizens. Women who succeed in television news have "made it" in a predominantly male field. That helps American women who are having a hard time being taken seriously. We are also examples for the girls and young women who will grow up unaware that women should expect any fewer professional opportunities than men.

We owe it to future generations of women to do our best, professionally and ethically. More and more women in television news are well known to the public, and while we're not celebrities in the Hollywood sense, we do have a well-defined public image. As long as women are measured against a higher standard of conduct than men, we have an obligation to be worthy of trust and to be honest because we are setting examples for women who follow us. And not only do we provide inspirations to younger *women,* but we also demonstrate to future generations of *men* that women can handle serious responsibilities if they're given the opportunities.

More Vast Than Wasteland:
The Influence of Television

As various political pundits became disillusioned with the prospect of choosing between Ronald Reagan and Jimmy Carter in 1980, picking the ideal candidate became a favorite parlor game. One frequently mentioned possibility was CBS anchorman Walter Cronkite. Cronkite certainly knew the issues, handicappers reasoned, since he had reported every major national political story over the past two decades. Moreover, he must be a pretty good indoor politician to have survived three decades of television network politics. And no one could question Cronkite's ability to inspire trust among voters; indeed, he was the most trusted figure in the country, according to some polls. *The New Republic,* the influential liberal magazine, reported that independent John Anderson was seriously considering Cronkite as a running mate, and others even floated the idea of drafting him for President.

The prospect struck some as preposterous. "Why in the world," one of his colleagues asked, "would Cronkite want to be President of the United States and give up all that power?" While that jesting remark may have overstated the case for the medium's clout a bit, the power television news wields is no joke. It affects the public, politics, and the broadcast industry itself.

About fifty million viewers watch the network news each

night. Some 64 percent of Americans say they get most of their information about what's going on in the world from television, according to a Roper survey in November 1980. And other public opinion surveys show that Americans consider TV news reports more credible than what they read in the newspapers. Those numbers add up to impact—both political and commercial. And it's because of this impact that politicians, especially presidents, sometimes make decisions, statements, or public appearances based on what they think TV's reaction or the reaction of TV's audience will be. Before he decided whether to make a speech, President Jimmy Carter frequently asked the networks whether they would broadcast it live. And every president prefers to schedule his televised addresses around popular TV programs rather than risk angering viewers by interrupting a regular broadcast of a favorite situation comedy or sports event.

The numbers also translate into ratings, which translate into profits for the networks. Even though each of the Big Three spends more than $30 million a year producing its evening news shows, the networks rake in $40,000 or more for every thirty-second ad, which more than offsets their expenditures. Not so long ago TV news shows were carried mainly to appease the Federal Communications Commission's public responsibility requirements. Today news is one of the most profitable areas of programming for networks, which is one reason why TV news is expanding. ABC has its "Nightline," NBC has "NBC News Overnight," and all three networks are expanding their morning news broadcasts and would like to increase their thirty minute evening newscast to a full hour.

So, while television news's influence is already enormous, it seems that it will become even greater with the expansion of network news and the advent of cable television news. And with this growing power has come a responsibility that is sobering. In my ten years as a broadcast journalist—six of them at the network level—I have found that it's a responsibility that TV news takes very seriously. But complicated questions remain about the implications of that responsibility in the face of television's growing power. And television's critics often oversimplify those questions. They attack the effect while either misunderstanding or ignoring the cause.

One of the most commonly heard complaints about TV news is that it is *too* powerful, that it can make or break a politician or a story. The defenders of the war in Vietnam, for example, accuse TV news coverage of undermining public support for America's involvement by sensationalizing the violence of that war. Ronald Reagan, who believes U.S. involvement in Vietnam in the 1960s and '70s was entirely appropriate, told *TV Guide* in early 1982 that TV news always wants to say "we're intervening." He charged TV news coverage with undermining his Administration's efforts to convince the American people of Soviet infiltration in Central America.

"There has been [in El Salvador] a kind of editorial slant that has something, almost, of the Vietnam syndrome, which challenges what we're doing there," Reagan said. "Vietnam was another example. I think the media had decided that the war was wrong. Had that been done in World War II, in behalf of the enemy that was killing American military men, I think there would have been a revolution in America."

But with all due respect to Mr. Reagan, his memory seems rather selective when it comes to Vietnam and El Salvador, and his estimation of the role TV news has played in these two instances is exaggerated. Certainly a greater factor contributing to the public's disillusionment with Vietnam was the U.S. government's repeated lies to its citizens about the war, lies which eventually began to unravel. As for El Salvador, TV news wasn't the only party raising serious doubts about purported Soviet infiltration. Nor was it the first to do so. Long before the Administration triggered daily network news coverage of El Salvador's civil war by sending in unarmed American military advisers, dissenters in the State Department and Congress criticized Reagan for a policy they said was meddlesome.

Still, the impression—however mistaken—exists that TV news intentionally manipulates public political opinion through its coverage of issues and events. And we in the business don't take that charge lightly. I think TV reporters tend to be far more self-critical and conscientious about maintaining balance than most of our critics realize. This is partly because broadcasting, unlike publishing, is a government-regulated industry, and partly because we are acutely aware of the power of television.

In evaluating TV's coverage of the conflict in El Salvador, for example, some network correspondents complained in a *Newsweek* magazine article that the only time they could get a story on the air was when it included videotape footage of "bang bang" (gunfire), and they were worried about the effect of this. "A few shots fired at a mango tree can be built into an ambush," said one correspondent, "if you get those shots on tape and the tape gets on the nightly news." These are the kinds of concerns we continually discuss and sometimes argue about. We *are* concerned about presenting stories fairly as well as accurately.

The notion of a powerful liberal bias in television that is skewing public opinion is contradicted by the fact that the country has plainly been moving in a more conservative direction in recent years. Republicans have captured three of the past four presidential elections, two of them by landslides. And one of the most knowledgeable students of TV's political coverage, Michael Robinson of George Washington University, says his research proves that TV's influence on the 1980 elections was actually *smaller* than it had been four years earlier.

Still, it's true that to the extent that television news—and all journalism—imposes order on random, chaotic events in condensing them into coherent and sometimes dramatic news stories, TV does shape the news. "None of us is content to let an event be an event," NBC's Roger Mudd told a Harvard University seminar on television and politics. "We have to fix it. We have to foreshorten the conclusions, hasten the end, predict before anyone else does who's going to win. We have to take an issue on our terms, and we won't let the candidate lay out the issues on his terms."

But this is not due to some sinister, intentional manipulation or a conspiracy to slant the news. Nor is it due to what some have described as the news media's liberal bias. It's the result of art attempting to imitate life, and of incredible competitive and deadline pressures. And it is a problem that is not unique to TV journalism.

To anyone who knows the highly competitive and sometimes cutthroat business of television news, the old Spiro Agnew-inspired notion that the networks—or the Eastern establishment press—sit down to plot the day's story line is ludicrous. Network executives sometimes seem ready to kill to beat their competitors on a story. In the close, cramped quarters of the White House, which you'd think would foster an esprit de corps among those who work there, reporters elbow each other out of the way during driveway stakeouts to make room for their camera crews. And the rivalry, no doubt, will become even fiercer if predictions prove correct that cable television and other technological advances will mean a decreasing share of viewers for the networks. One New York advertising agency recently estimated a 24 percent decline in network audiences by 1990. Thus, the Big Three are worrying about survival, a concern that doesn't lend itself to boardroom conspiracies to plot like approaches to news coverage.

It is not network executives, however, who are responsible

for a problem that does exist among reporters who make it to the top in Washington. Others mistakenly call it an Eastern establishment bias: I believe it is, more correctly, a loss of perspective. As a group, we have more in common with highly paid businesspeople than with the average person scratching for a living wage. We do not spend our time among average folks, and don't share many of the community and city problems they do. Most of us care deeply about those real problems, but we live in a company town, isolated from the rest of the country, and we spend more time talking about the Secretary of State's latest shuttle than we do high property taxes.

The problem becomes evident when the national media dispatch their reporters on whistlestop tours of the hinterlands to do those "mood of the country" stories. In television's case, we stick a microphone in the face of some steelworker or housewife and, presto, we have a symbol of working-class America, or, even more ludicrous, the inside track on what the country is *really* thinking. It's always seemed to me that there is something a little patronizing about the way we do these man-on-the-street interviews.

The bias issue confronts news announcers on a different level as well. John Chancellor told an interviewer he had to work hard to make his voice "neutral." "It's a skill," he said, "and we ought to be good at it."

Another criticism often aimed at television news is that six-figure-salary-fueled egos are more and more becoming participants in the events they cover, instead of being content merely to observe them from the reporting sidelines. Reuven Frank, president of NBC News, has deplored what he describes as "the rise of the reporter as institution."

More troubling than overweening egos is the effect of celebrity. While there's no doubt that the wages of fame can be heady—Dan Rather earns a reported yearly $2,000,000; Barbara Walters, $1,300,000; Tom Brokaw, $1,200,000—

they can also be a headache. I once saw Walter Cronkite follow Jimmy Carter into a five-and-dime store in Nashua, New Hampshire, during a 1976 campaign stop, and emerge with more fans trailing after him than Carter did. Unfortunately for Cronkite, he was not running against Carter; he was trying to cover him. And he looked less than thrilled to be doing his job with an entourage underfoot. It's a problem just about every well-known TV news anchor has to contend with, and it makes it exceedingly difficult for them to cover stories in the field, which is probably why they don't do more of it. It's unfortunate because the news anchors are some of the best and most experienced reporters in the business or they wouldn't be where they are.

Television is also accused of being a captive of pictures and a slave to the ratings, more concerned about what the news looks like and what the audience share is than about reporting.

This is preposterous. No network news executive could last in this business if he tried to cover stories, or change them, on the basis of ratings. It simply is not the way news works. It is as crazy as the idea that the *New York Times* or the *Washington Post* or the *Wall Street Journal* cover stories to increase circulation. Having said that, I will not deny that some local television news operations cover sensational crime stories or zany "events" to boost their ratings.

It is true that we in network news discuss the ratings, and if we dwell on them too much, I suspect that we do so because they are the only tangible proof of how we stack up against our competitors. It's been said of newspapers that today's edition is tomorrow's fish wrap. But in TV news the results of our efforts disappear into the air. In a sense, the ratings are a way of calling them back.

And of course each of those ratings points also translates into a great deal of money. Broadcasting is a business as well as a public medium. Former CBS News president Bill Leonard said, "We exist in between the pages of a business . . . that is primarily successful because it is the greatest means of mass medium entertainment ever invented.

"That is fundamentally what the business is all about, and it is fundamentally what supports most of it. We [in TV news] exist alternately with that, and sometimes we are confused by that. I think it is a tribute, actually, to the management of all three networks that they have insisted, over all this quarter of a century, that we are important, that we be allowed to flourish, that we be given the resources to flourish."

But even though the ratings don't affect network news decisions about what to put on the air or how to play it, they obviously do affect decisions about *who* to put on the air. Network anchorpeople rise and fall at a jump or a drop in the ratings. And one CBS news executive reportedly even went so far as to order more air-time for prominent correspondents during CBS News's battle to retain its rating dominance just after Dan Rather succeeded Walter Cronkite. That order, which was leaked in a memo, was seized on by some as a dangerous precedent that could lead to deciding what news was based on who was covering it. I dislike the implications, even though I frankly don't believe there is any danger of a network news show opting for an all-star cast over a strong story lineup. It just doesn't jibe with the competitive nature of the news business. What's more, those prominent CBS correspondents are among the network's best reporters.

While we do have our faults in the way we sometimes present stories—using overly jazzy visual effects, or simplifying by going for the personality or the sensational in a story when we should be explaining complexity—refusing to cover an important news development because it lacks good visuals just isn't one of them. One proof of that is the regularity with which White House stories, probably the most consistently boring stories of all from a visual standpoint, appear on the air. A White House report makes the news most every night, sometimes with nothing better to illustrate it than a picture of the president in a meeting and a correspondent's stand-up on the lawn. And while we try to use interesting visuals to enliven essentially dull, dry stories, you can't argue that White House coverage is exciting television.

Making stories visually interesting is an important consideration in our business, and that sometimes means marginal stories don't get on the air. And the conflict between making a story interesting and simply telling it causes some in the business to chafe. "The basic problem is the conflict between being an honest reporter and being a member of show business," says Roger Mudd, "and that conflict is with us every day. If you are dedicated to honest, unaffected, untrammeled reporting, you run up against the demands of making the news that evening interesting."

Bill Leonard sees the conflict as that of a young medium still coming to terms with itself. "We're trapped by our origins, which came from print, and we're not sure just where we fit in in relation to that," he said. "We're a little bit trapped by our origins from radio. We don't know quite whether we're a form of print translated . . . into pictures, or a form of pictures that comes from radio—we don't yet quite know who and what we are in television."

One of the most serious criticisms leveled at television is that we have destroyed political parties and political conventions, and generally set back the electoral and governing processes in the country. Distinguished political observer Austin Ranney, former president of the American Political Science Association, this year told *The Washington Post* that the television networks make it harder for presidents to govern: "They accelerate political consciousness and feed an impatience for quick results, no matter how complex the problems. They want things solved in sixty minutes—less commercials. If the Civil War had been fought in the television age, I have no doubt there would be an independent Confederate States of America today, because that was a mismanaged, bungled operation (by the Union) almost until the end."

The medium's penchant for transitory political coverage is an inherent problem, as Bill Moyers sees it. "Politicians deal in a world of complexity, and television deals in a world of simplicity," Moyers said. I agree: Most ninety-second news spots don't lend themselves to complicated or thoughtful examinations of any subject. Moreover, I think there are times when TV goes overboard in covering politics, especially conventions. CBS's coverage of the 1980 GOP convention overstepped the bounds of reporting, I think, when it permitted anchorman Walter Cronkite to get carried away with speculating on a Reagan-Ford ticket during a televised interview with Gerald Ford. "As both men fell prey to euphoric extravagance, acting as if they were about to take the decision into their own hands," recalled Jonathan Moore of Harvard's Institute of Politics, Ronald Reagan watched it all on his TV set with the rest of the country.

Following the 1980 elections NBC was criticized for declaring Reagan the winner a few hours before the California polls closed on election night. I think early projections are proper, if based on thorough and responsible research, as NBC's were. I'm also aware that such early calls *may* have an effect on later voting habits, and that concerns me. But in the 1980 elections I think that Jimmy Carter's early concession, which was based on projections by his own people, was far more influential than NBC's early announcement of a winner. Once they knew that the presidential election was lost, some wavering Democratic voters might have stayed home, and that probably hurt other Democratic candidates in their races.

Congressman Jim Corman, an influential House Democrat from Los Angeles, was defeated by only 752 votes out of 150,000 cast.

While there are valid questions about television's impact on politics, I still think much of the criticism is quite exaggerated. As the country has become increasingly disillusioned with its choice of political candidates, I think there is a tendency to overly romanticize what political parties used to be and the role they played in selecting candidates. Often, these choices were made in smoke-filled back rooms by political bosses who delivered precinct votes in exchange for promises of political favors.

The erosion in the parties' power began before television. As historian Arthur Schlesinger has pointed out, this process has been evolving for most of the twentieth century. The decline in immigration, which deprived political organizations of their classic clientele; the rise of civil service, which limited patronage; and the New Deal's taking over much of the welfare role, Schlesinger says, have all contributed to the decline of political parties.

The notion that political campaigns were more uplifting before television is also suspect. "If we look at history," says Johnson White House Press Secretary George Reedy, "we're going to find that in the long run of American politics, issues have been settled over such profound things as, 'Ma, ma, where's my pa? Gone to the White House, ha, ha.' Or the very deep analysis of our problems with Canada, 'Fifty-four-Forty or Fight.' Or, when I was a child, the mayor of Chicago ran a very successful campaign on the slogan that he would take the first boat to England and punch King George in the snoot." All of this before television entered the fray.

There are positive points here, too. Television has opened up the political process. Voters no longer need local party leaders to tell them about candidates. On-the-scene coverage allows the public to hear a candidate's promises for themselves and to see the reaction to that message as he stumps along on the campaign trail. This, I believe, has helped make elected officials more accountable to the public. It's also more difficult now for candidates to flip-flop on the issues once they're elected. A president who changes positions on an issue, as Reagan did on the balanced budget, finds that TV will run old clips of previous statements.

We have also made strides in the quality of coverage. For instance, ten years ago TV's coverage of economics consisted of "a quick glance at the Dow Jones closing average before the final commercial on the evening news," complained former Treasury Undersecretary Charls Walker. The built-in lack of interesting visuals to illustrate these stories, coupled with the notable dearth of economic specialists in TV news, made the economy one of the most short-shrifted areas of network news coverage. Today, Walker sees enormous improvements in TV's economic coverage. Each of the networks has at least one economic or business expert as fully qualified as their print colleagues. NBC has Irving R. Levine in Washington and Mike Jensen in New York; CBS has George Herman, and ABC has Dan Cordtz.

It's not unusual for economic news to lead the evening shows these days, with accompanying "sidebar" pieces on the impact of a particular economic development. And we have learned to make economic news visually interesting, without compromising its substance, through improved technology and video libraries. Instead of talking heads delivering the economic news, "chyrons" and "quantels" of numbers flashing on the screen, videotape clips of supermarket checkout counters, houses under construction, or the floor of the New York Stock Exchange help tell the story.

Economics isn't the only area where TV's coverage has improved. Beats such as the Supreme Court, energy, environment, and science, all feature expert reporters. A few years ago, nearly all TV reporters were generalists. Today, they are much more specialized. It's not unusual for these news specialists to have graduate degrees in their areas of expertise or extensive newspaper reporting experience before joining a network.

I think television's political coverage has improved also, given the constraints of time on the air. We are broadcasting more special reports on serious issues, as well as examining them through multiple-part series during regular newscasts. In addition, television is beginning to provide a window on the legislative process itself. TV's live, continuous coverage of the proceedings in the House of Representatives, I believe, is an important first step in broadening political coverage. And while some initially worried that television would intrude more than it would elucidate, Senate Majority Leader Howard Baker, who advocates opening his chamber's doors to TV, believes that experience has refuted those concerns. "Early fears that members would be intimidated or bedazzled by the television cameras in their midst have by and large been proved groundless," Baker says. "Showmanship has not run amok in the House, nor have its members run off in droves to sign up for acting or locution lessons."

No news organization in the world can mobilize resources faster to report, live, the assassination of a Sadat, the shooting of a President, or almost any other breaking story. And now, we are learning to examine the causes and the effects of news developments as well. Still, I believe our biggest mistake is not that we try too hard to be first with the news but that we're sometimes content to be second. Too often, we're not willing to broadcast stories until they have first apeared in the newspapers, particularly the front page of the *New York Times*.

My colleague Marvin Kalb, NBC's diplomatic correspondent, recalls that when he was with CBS and couldn't get certain stories on "Evening News," he would often give them to the *Times*. Then he was frequently asked to do a second-day story for the network. (Much of the clout of the *Times*, only the fourth largest paper in the country, rests with the impact it has on TV news executives, all of whom live in New York.) Public Broadcasting's Robert McNeil argues that because of an "historical inferiority complex" television's political coverage always has been "to a large degree derivative of what is in the print press." Or, as columnist Mark Shields suggests, "Television dominates the dialogue in American politics but print sets the agenda." I think television is slowly shedding this inferiority complex, and as we gain more confidence the result will be better and more timely coverage.

Television's power is so often viewed as a negative force in our lives and in society that we tend to overlook the contributions it has made. Besides being the greatest mass medium of entertainment ever invented, it is the greatest mass communicator. TV has played a major role in informing and educating us—as individuals and as a society. It has comforted a shocked nation in the aftermath of one president's assassination and another's shooting. It has rejoiced with us at America's moon landing and space shots.

Television's coverage of the civil rights marches, with its vivid pictures of Southern sheriffs unleashing vicious dogs or overpowering water hoses on blacks, helped persuade a nation that had once enslaved blacks that discriminating against blacks was unjust. And TV's reporting on the peace process in the Middle East played a unifying role in bringing together Israel's Menachem Begin and Egypt's Anwar Sadat at Camp David and later in Jerusalem.

Moreover, television news has produced some extraordinary talented professionals. The fashionable notion that television news is dominated by cliche-happy bubbleheads is nonsense— at least on the network level. The people who make it to the top, almost without exception, really are the best in television journalism. Even discounting my bias, for example, the last three anchormen for my network—John Chancellor, Roger Mudd, and Thomas Brokaw—are excellent journalists.

As television evolves, it appears that its contributions will increase along with its power. Improvements in over-the-air broadcasting through the use of satellites, combined with innovations in cable technology, are expected to transform television into a catalogue of consumer information and services. Banking, shopping, and even mail delivery will be done electronically by television. Teachers and professors will be brought to their students through television, instead of the students' having to go to classes. Research centers—from the Library of Congress to newspaper clip files—will be accessible by simply pressing a few buttons on your TV sets. But perhaps the biggest change in the future will be the expansion and improvement of TV programming from broadcasting to "narrowcasting," as some have termed the rise of special-interest programming in television. There will be channels for children, sports fans, opera and theater buffs, and film freaks—a virtual satellite and cable "jukebox" of entertainment selections from which viewers may pick and choose.

Even more important than this wider selection in TV entertainment, however, will be a concomitant wider selection in TV news. Until now the network newscasts have been the "gatekeeper" for the American public, "determining the agenda of the nation," in the view of former FCC chairman Charles Ferris, through a limited number of news programs and a limited amount of time in which to present them. Ferris predicts that as the public's appetite for news increases, the amount of news programming carried by the networks will increase and the competition among them will grow more intense. New operations, such as all-news cable networks, will add to the competition. The current expansion of network newscasts and the networks' realization that their news strength is their ability to broadcast, within a matter of minutes, breaking news events from virtually every corner of the globe, Ferris says, will inevitably lead to more news programming by the networks.

Expanding the time devoted to news gathering and broadcasting can only improve the quality of TV news coverage. Increasingly in our daily coverage we'll be challenging newspapers in such areas as long, in-depth stories, behind-the-scenes reports, and so-called "think pieces" on current issues, in addition to the live coverage we already do better. More news programming will also mean more opportunities to do followup stories, and less opportunities for politicians to manipulate their television news coverage by playing on our deadlines. Public television's McNeil-Lehrer Report has vividly demonstrated that television can air informative *and* interesting discussions of serious issues every night.

But even though the networks will be broadcasting more news, they will be competing for a shrinking audience. Cable TV, with its potential selection of eighty channels, is expected to reach at least 50 percent of the TV homes in the country by the end of the decade, and predictions are that the networks' audience share will drop from the current 80 percent to 60 percent by the end of the century. The expected result of this will be that the public will no longer depend exclusively on the three networks as the major source of information and news. The vast majority of Americans will no longer share identical information, but will have a much wider spectrum of news coverage from which to choose. With an entertainment jukebox of more than eighty channels to select from, coupled with a proliferation in videotape recorders, some Americans may even tune news out of their lives altogether.

Charles Ferris sees this as a potentially revolutionary change in how the public will view government and its leaders. He predicts that the end of the network news monopoly will alter society's opinions of its leaders and the world around us. As a result, leaders' capacity to rule will change a great deal.

There will be many more perceptions out there about what happened—in the political arena and elsewhere.

Today, if the President decides to raise taxes and makes a televised speech to explain his decision, 90 percent of the public with TV in their homes will hear his explanation, because all three networks will carry the President's speech simultaneously. But if the public has access to 100 different channels and only, say, 7 percent of the public watches the President's speech, the political dynamics change. But exactly how those dynamics will change no one knows. Will the public turn to one of the all-news channels for more information, an instant analysis of the speech, or a reaction from other political officials for a broader view of the President's decision? Or will they tune him out? In either case, the proliferation of TV programming will have an impact on the coalescing of national attitudes about significant issues of the day. And it will be far more difficult for politicians to manipulate those attitudes. Ferris likens the resulting diversity in the public's perception about major events of the day to the situation existing in the pre-television era.

There is also a troubling aspect to the new TV technology in terms of how it will affect the potential role television will play in shaping those national attitudes and possibly even government policy. Two-way cable TV installations are already experimenting with "instant" polling of the public on questions of public policy. It may be possible in the future to conduct daily referenda on important national issues. And that could lead democracy to a dangerous extreme: policy decision-making based on whatever information could be made quickly available, without thoughtful consideration of the ramifications over the longer run. The "whimsical nature" of such polls, Ferris says, "could undermine the whole notion of a republican form of government."

We saw an ominous harbinger of such an eventuality following the presidential campaign debate between Ronald

Reagan and Jimmy Carter on the eve of the 1980 election. ABC offered two phone numbers which viewers could call to say who they thought won the debate. It cost fifty cents to call, and the instant poll showed Reagan was preferred by about a two-to-one margin. Most public-opinion experts and journalists thought this technique was slanted—more Republicans have telephones and they are generally somewhat wealthier—as well as journalistically irresponsible.

So even with the proliferation of information sources, there is no guarantee that we, the people, will make better judgments as a consequence. All we can say for sure is that we'll have more information and the ability to act more quickly in response to it. And, in a broader sense, this TV communications revolution will surely raise new, troubling questions for society as a whole. In short, how can a self-governing people master, rather than be mastered by, electronic technology?

Ferris worries that the future "may have a dark side," in terms of how government will respond to TV's increasing power. He asked if, on the one hand, we could afford to tell the government, "Hands off," and still expect a free, open communications marketplace. On the other hand, can we give the government a role in regulating television, yet somehow manage to prevent government from controlling it like some Orwellian Big Brother?

The potential abuses of individual privacy is another serious problem in TV's future, as people plug into their banks and offices via their TV sets. What would stop the cable TV company, or the government, Ferris asks, from learning the net worth of 250 million Americans?

He believes the potential for such invasions of privacy must be curbed now, before the new technology is installed in homes. Otherwise, the government's inclination might be to collect all the information it could and ask questions later about what is appropriate to store.

Whatever curbs society chooses to impose on government's access to the private records of its citizens, a number of questions will have to be answered first. Should the government have *any* access? If so, to what? And who in the government will get the information?

The growth of pay TV also leads some to wonder whether the poor will be excluded from the cream of the TV programming being offered. Les Brown, editor of *Channels* magazine, worries that TV's new public-access channels and computer information banks "will only increase the gap between rich and poor by dividing a single national constituency into two nations: one information-rich and able to participate and influence the national destiny more effectively than ever before, the other information-poor, relegated to still greater powerlessness." If television's new technology is to help realize the ideal of an active, informed citizenry, Brown says, it will have to be offered at a minimal cost to all Americans.

Changes in technology and the increase in TV news sources will mean an even more pressing need for self-examination. Today, all reporters do a poor job of covering—and policing—ourselves. Former White House Press Secretary Jody Powell has said that he'd like to see the networks forced to answer tough questions about how they got and played a story. He suggested that if one network blows a story, another should investigate how and why it happened. As Tom Johnson, the publisher of the *Los Angeles Times* and a former aide to President Lyndon Johnson, put it, "We exempt ourselves from accountability, while demanding it of others. We hold too much power for that."

I think we have a responsibility, as we expand our news time-slots, to do more of this kind of self-examination. And I think we should make the penalties for errors in reporting more severe. We owe it to our viewers, and we owe it to ourselves.

Index

Index

Index